Your Deal, Mr. Bond

Phillip and Robert King

B. T. Batsford Ltd, *London*

First published 1997

© Phillip and Robert King 1997

ISBN 0 7134 8247 8

Typeset by Apsbridge Services Ltd, Nottingham.

Printed by Redwood Books, Trowbridge, Wiltshire
for the publishers,
B. T. Batsford Ltd, 583 Fulham Road,
London SW6 5BY

A BATSFORD BRIDGE BOOK
Series Editor: Tony Sowter

CONTENTS

FOREWORD

When reviewing the Kings' earlier works, I advised my readers to buy them as Christmas presents, but to be sure to read them first. I then told Phillip and Robert that their following effort, *Farewell My Dummy*, was one of the best bridge books I had read. And before I knew it, I had talked myself into agreeing to write an introduction to *Your Deal Mr Bond*.

Then I discovered that I actually appeared in it as a character, and it was too late to prevent it. Still, I reflected, not many people can say that they have been cast as James Bond's back-up man in a fight to save Western civilisation. I can't wait for the film to come out.

All three stories are well up to the author's high standards, and the deals are well up to mine. As usual, the humour enhances the bridge and the bridge enhances the humour. For example, the Frankenstein piece cleverly employs black comedy to define the qualities of the perfect bridge player. And *Some Might Get Shot* evokes the ultimate male bridge fantasy – being squeezed by Marilyn Monroe.

The Bridge World recently advised "P & R, keep them coming." I am delighted to have helped them to do so.

Zia Mahmood

INTRODUCTION

Our fourth volume of bridge fiction differs from the other three in that only the title story, *Your Deal, Mr Bond*, is a parody.

In *Frankenstein's Bridge Partner*, for example, we have borrowed the name of Mary Shelley's character, and his favourite hobby, but little else. Our main debt of gratitude is to Tony Forrester, for his co-operation with a vital aspect of the plot. Without it, a happy ending would have been impossible.

For the very young, it may be necessary to point out that *Some Might Get Shot* is a tribute to the 1959 movie, *Some Like It Hot*, which starred Marilyn Monroe, Tony Curtis and Jack Lemmon. The screenplay, by Billy Wilder and I.A.L. Diamond, was not based on any existing prose work, so it was easier to parody the plot than the style. The two cross-dressing musicians become bridge pros, and the action has been brought forward, from 1929 to the mid-1930s, when the bridge craze was at its peak.

We would like to acknowledge the editorial skills of Su Burn. She must take credit for much of the hard work, and (we are generous enough to admit it) all of the mistakes.

Finally we wish to express our special thanks to Zia, both for his encouragement, and his unique contribution to *Your Deal, Mr Bond*.

1
SOME MIGHT GET SHOT

Jack Melon surveyed the dummy with an air of confidence he didn't feel. "Thank you, partner," he said, while inwardly cursing Tony's chronic speech impediment. The klutz couldn't bring himself to say pass.

It was just a no-account pairs event in New York, but they were bridge pros, with reputations to guard and clients to impress. In the round before the interval, they were on parade before two little old widows from Vermont. Mrs Dupont and Mrs Havermeyer were as rich as six feet down in Iowa, and they smiled sweetly while they spanked you with wickedly close doubles and sneaky defences.

The diamond slam had as much chance as a one-legged man in a butt-kicking contest. And even if Jack performed his regulation miracle, the serial overbidder opposite would just grin like a Pepsodent ad and say, "I knew you'd make it, partner."

Jack gritted his teeth and wondered, for the hundredth time playing with Tony, why it was called gritting.

Game All. Dealer South.

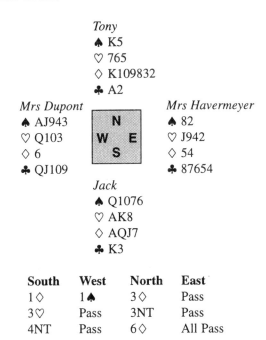

Tony
♠ K5
♡ 765
◇ K109832
♣ A2

Mrs Dupont
♠ AJ943
♡ Q103
◇ 6
♣ QJ109

Mrs Havermeyer
♠ 82
♡ J942
◇ 54
♣ 87654

Jack
♠ Q1076
♡ AK8
◇ AQJ7
♣ K3

South	West	North	East
1◇	1♠	3◇	Pass
3♡	Pass	3NT	Pass
4NT	Pass	6◇	All Pass

Jack noted Mrs Dupont's ♣Q lead, and paused like a true pro as he tried to figure the distribution. Judging by her overcall, and her cute little smile when she saw the dummy, he'd lay odds she held the ace and jack of spades as well as the guarded queen of hearts.

When he called for the ♣A, little Mrs Havermeyer produced the four. This was a partnership way ahead of its time – they gave count. So it looked like she had a five-card suit.

Jack drew trumps. Mrs Dupont showed out. Now he could place her with a 5-3-1-4 shape. Maybe 6-2-1-4, in which case he could cash his top hearts and the club ace. Then, if he played on spades, she would be endplayed into conceding the twelfth trick.

But no, she had that smug look of a woman who knew that her man was about to go down, so he would play her for ♡Qxx. He advanced the ♠10, which was covered by the jack and king. A second round drew the eight from little Mrs Havermeyer, and Jack's queen forced the ace. Now the stage was set to take a ruffing finesse against the spade nine, and a well-earned bow.

"Nicely done, young man." Mrs Dupont beamed at Jack as if she liked his modest build and neurotic manner as much as his smooth card play. Then she turned to Tony Citrus, Tony the charmer, so good-looking he wasn't real. "But as for you, young man, bidding like yours ought to be a federal offence."

This was par for the course. Old ladies always preferred Jack to Tony. It was as if the two of them had divided womankind down the middle and poor Tony was stuck with the younger half. But the gleam in his eye as it lit on Mrs Dupont's three-tier pearl necklace showed he hadn't yet conceded the geriatric vote.

"I could live with that, ma'am." He flashed a set of teeth pearlier than her necklace. "Provided you were the arresting officer."

Mrs Dupont sniffed disdainfully, while little Mrs Havermeyer cleared her throat. This was her way of asking permission to speak, and Mrs Dupont granted it with a regal nod.

"Gentlemen," said Mrs Havermeyer, "I'm told you play for money."

"It has been known, ma'am," replied Tony, who always took the lead in financial matters. "We do not support the theory that good bridge players are born and not paid. Had you a few high-stake rubbers in mind? We also give lessons – not that you need them of course, but our terms are extremely reasonable."

Mrs Dupont coughed, to indicate that Mrs Havermeyer had used up her verbal ration. "What my friend wishes to say is that we are going to Florida for the bridge congress which starts this weekend, and we are looking for two good ladies to make up the team."

"Well as you can see," said Tony, "we are good players, but somewhat lacking in the other department."

"But perhaps you know a couple of nice girls who would appreciate two weeks of luxury, all paid for, and maybe a little spending money."

"How little?"

"If they are really fine players, two hundred a piece." Mrs Dupont took a card from her purse and gave it to Jack. "If you should think of someone, we are staying at the Waldorf."

They picked up their cards for the next board and Tony smiled at Jack. "By the way, partner," he said, "I knew you'd make it."

2

Times were very tough indeed for Spats Coleano. Being the Southside rackets boss in the depression was no bed of roses. The weekly take was down. The Syndicate's cut was up. And now there was border trouble with Big Vinny from the Northside.

Which is why Spats lurked in the shadows of the parking lot behind the McKinley building, and waited to give Big Vinny some tips on local geography. With Spats were Danny the Ox and Fingers Flannery, and he hoped their three machine guns would ram home the lesson without the need for anything drastic, like a blackboard and chalk.

A driver was sitting at the wheel of Big Vinny's bullet-proof Cadillac, waiting uncomplainingly for his boss to return. It was difficult to complain when your throat was cut and the only thing holding you upright was a coil of rope.

Spats shivered, and cast his mind back to that cold morning years ago in Brooklyn, the morning which had taught him that crime paid. A little orphan boy was walking the streets wondering how to get money to buy medicine for his sick grandmother, when he found a five dollar bill on the sidewalk. Then, as he closed his eyes in a silent prayer of thanks, a hoodlum busted his nose, grabbed the five bucks, broke his jaw for good measure, and got clean away.

It was a lesson Spats never forgot, for he was that hoodlum.

♦ ♦ ♦ ♦ ♦

Meanwhile, Tony was giving Mrs Dupont a lesson in non-violent defence.

Game All. Dealer South.

Mrs Havermeyer
♠ K5
♡ 1098
◇ K9765
♣ A108

Tony
♠ 432
♡ A76
◇ Q32
♣ Q543

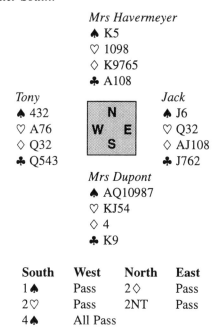

Jack
♠ J6
♡ Q32
◇ AJ108
♣ J762

Mrs Dupont
♠ AQ10987
♡ KJ54
◇ 4
♣ K9

South	West	North	East
1♠	Pass	2◇	Pass
2♡	Pass	2NT	Pass
4♠	All Pass		

At several tables, West had decided to attack the unbid suit. The lead of the ♣3 had given declarer a milk run to twelve tricks when East unwisely contributed the jack. Against Mrs Dupont, Tony led the ♣Q.

As soon as Mrs Dupont saw this card, she was hell-bent on getting a cheap top. She won in hand and smartly finessed the ♣10. Her groan when this lost to the jack could be heard four tables away. After taking the trick, Jack cashed his ◇A and exited with the ♠J. Mrs Dupont discarded hearts on dummy's two minor suit winners, and now had to guess the hearts for the contract. Since she did not want the ♡Q to be onside she played a heart to the king.

As Mrs Dupont recorded her unique minus, she gave Tony a look of reluctant admiration. "So you're not just a pretty face," she murmured thoughtfully.

"It wasn't difficult, ma'am. The bidding showed that you had ten cards in the majors. The lead of the queen often gains in those situations." He stood up and bowed. This was a rare gesture in Manhattan, but there was a rumour that people still did it in Vermont. "Please excuse us, ladies. We like to go out for a smoke during the interval."

"You'll know why when you've tasted the coffee," said Jack.

They took the stairs to the back entrance of the McKinley building and slipped into the parking lot. They sat on the fender of a nearby Packard and lit cigarettes.

It turned out to be the most ill-fated smoke of their lives.

The set up was perfect, thought Spats. The only thing going on at the McKinley was bridge, and nothing short of an earthquake coinciding with a routine partscore would drag bridge players away from the table.

Spats had played a little bridge. The whole country was caught up in the craze, and where there was a craze there was dough. One day he would see if the game needed organizing, but that would have to wait, because two big gorillas were heading his way, followed by Big Vinny. As they reached their bullet-proof Cadillac, the dead look on the driver's face told them they'd forgotten to make it razor-proof. Three hands began a hopeful journey towards their shoulders, but froze at the sound of Spats' voice.

"Hold it, Vinny!" Spats stepped out from the shadows. He was a sharp dresser, with a hard, handsome face and slicked-back hair as dark as two yards up a chimney. His very presence commanded respect. Or maybe it was the tommy gun. Danny and Fingers appeared, and Vinny was looking at enough fire power to storm the Alamo.

"Be reasonable, Spats." Vinny's voice rasped from a throat that had turned as dry as a Martini with no vermouth. "Let's talk this thing over."

"What thing, Vinny?" Spats was having a ball. He felt like a man holding the ace of trumps when his opponents had bid a grand slam. "Could it be the little matter of where Northside ends and the South begins?"

"That's it, Spats. I guess a few of my boys have beeen getting too big for their boots."

"Much too big, Vinny. Maybe you should chop off a few toes."

"Sure thing, Spats. I'll have words with them." Vinny edged forward till his fat body masked his two big torpedoes, the fastest guns in town.

"Swell idea, Vinny. Tell 'em about the bad things that will happen if their map-reading don't improve more than somewhat."

"What bad things, Spats?" Vinny got ready to throw himself onto the ground to give his gunners a clear line of fire.

"I'll give you a clue, Vinny." Three tommy guns barked as one. Within five seconds Big Vinny's territorial ambitions had vanished in a torrent of lead, and the two fastest guns in town were still in their holsters.

"Start the car, Danny." Spats inspected the bodies with a steel patent-leather toe. They were as dead as three soused herrings. A good evening's work, he thought, until he heard a sound from behind an old Packard. He was about to check it out, when two young guys sprang from cover and made a frantic dash towards the McKinley. Before Spats could take aim, a door opened and they were lost in a group of people coming out.

Spats and Fingers ran to join Danny the Ox in the armour-plated Hispano Suiza. It turned into the street and headed South.

"What about them two guys, boss?" Fingers asked nervously.

"Bridge players," said Spats. "Pros. I sometimes see 'em around."

"Do you think they know you?"

Spats shrugged. "If I see 'em around, they see me around."

Danny gazed at him through the glazed eyes of a man who had played too much football without a helmet. "You want me to rub 'em out, boss?"

"Not tonight, Danny." Spats was ice cool. "They're bridge bums. They can't hide nowhere."

♦ ♦ ♦ ♦ ♦

"Do you think he recognised us?" Tony was the first to get his breath, probably because he got more exercise, such as giving the cards an extra shuffle.

"He knew me alright." Jack's face looked as if it would take major surgery to bring the colour back. "I once smacked his partner eleven hundred for a dumb five clubs sacrifice."

"It was your double that was dumb, Jack. You're lucky Spats didn't kill you."

"Yeah, but his partner hasn't been seen since. Tony, let's get out of here!"

"Don't panic." Tony spoke with the assurance of a man who knew his looks and charm could get him out of any spot. "We're quite safe."

"Are you kidding?"

"Any time now this place will be crawling with cops. We've got nothing to worry about until tomorrow."

"Well do you mind if I start now?"

"Relax, Jack. Tomorrow we're leaving town."

"In cement overcoats. And even if we get away, Spats is with the Syndicate. They'll be looking for us in every bridge club in the country."

"But they won't find us."

"In a pig's ear they won't. Bridge is our living. It's all we know."

"Don't worry, Jack. Just watch me." Tony led his friend to the table where the Vermont widows were taking their coffee.

"Ladies," he said. "We have just remembered two experts who will make you perfect team-mates. Our twin sisters."

3

"Antonia" and "Jacqueline" met their new team-mates on the station platform. Their clothes were provided by Tony's tallest girlfriend, and altered by Jack's homeliest. Wigs and make-up were by courtesy of a female impersonator in Greenwich Village. All in all, they could have looked worse. Not that they expected a chorus of wolf whistles, but, on a dark night, in a navy base full of short-sighted sailors, you never knew your luck.

Anyway, Mrs Dupont seemed satisfied with them, and as usual little Mrs Havermeyer followed her lead. They were soon travelling South, in the luxury of the widows' state room, and playing a rubber of bridge.

Tony partnered Mrs Dupont. Remembering her dislike of overbidders, he made a good start by turning down her invitation to a fifty-fifty game. He was rewarded by her beam of approval when a razor-sharp defence by Jack held her to nine tricks. Emboldened by this success, he stopped in two no trumps on the next deal. He had to produce a master play to avoid making an overtrick, but only Jack noticed the brilliancy.

"Well stopped, Antonia," Mrs Dupont purred. "Two bites at the cherry are often best."

On the next deal Tony was given the chance to transform her approval into undiluted worship.

Love All. Dealer North.

Mrs Dupont
♠ AKQJ
♡ AKJ
◇ AKQ
♣ K43

Mrs Havermeyer
♠ 543
♡ 10985
◇ 876
♣ A92

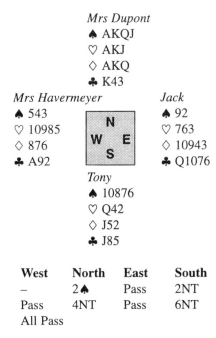

Jack
♠ 92
♡ 763
◇ 10943
♣ Q1076

Tony
♠ 10876
♡ Q42
◇ J52
♣ J85

West	North	East	South
–	2♠	Pass	2NT
Pass	4NT	Pass	6NT
All Pass			

Mrs Dupont favoured a simple bidding system with no frills, and Tony had quickly realised that getting her to change it would be like getting Custer's widow to sponsor a monument to Crazy Horse.

She opened a Culbertson forcing two spades, and showed the quality of her rock-crusher by a natural four no trump rebid. Tony's scattered values were beginning to look good. He knew he should stay in his partner's good books by passing cravenly, but the habits of a lifetime were too tough to break.

"Six no trumps," he cooed, in a beautifully modulated contralto.

Little Mrs Havermeyer led the ♡10, and Mrs Dupont tabled her cards proudly. Tony stared in agonised disbelief at the appalling duplication. The only hope seemed to be a doubleton ♣AQ on his left. But Tony didn't believe in Santa Claus, so he decided on a spot of grand larceny. He captured the first trick on the table, dropping the ♡4 from hand, and smoothly led the ♣K!

This went round to Mrs Havermeyer, who noted her partner's ♣7, and placed her with a doubleton, and declarer with ♣QJ1085 and no other entry. So she ducked expertly.

Tony's next move was to sneak a low club to his knave. Mrs Havermeyer saw no reason to change her expert strategy. She ducked again! Tony gratefully gathered his second trick, and fluttered his eyelids modestly as he laid down the other ten.

"Partner!" Mrs Dupont was open-mouthed. "That was the best played hand I've ever seen."

"She's got a million of them," said Jack, who was kicking himself for not rising with the ♣Q at trick three.

Mrs Havermeyer fixed more Martinis, while Mrs Dupont sat back like a cat that had just swallowed the cream.

"Well, girls." Mrs Dupont took a cigarette from a case which Jack priced at five years rent for their rooms in a Bronx tenement. "I must admit you are all your brothers said you were."

"Want to bet?" Jack muttered.

"I hope we can take that as a compliment," said Tony.

"Of course you can, Antonia," said Mrs Dupont. "And I'm pleased to say you don't bid rashly like your brother."

"No ma'am." Tony took a ladylike sip from his Martini. "He warned me about that."

"But otherwise you play just like him. You sit like him, you hold your cards like him ... Doesn't she, Ruby?"

Mrs Havermeyer cleared her throat and turned a smiling face to Jack. "She does indeed. And you too, Jacqueline, are just like *your* brother."

"Of course." Jack's falsetto giggle edged towards hysteria. "We're both identical twins. That's how we met – at a twins' convention."

"That's a new one on me." Mrs Dupont gave one of her most sardonic sniffs. "I know the Four no trumps convention and the Two Clubs convention. But the Twins convention? Have you heard of it, Ruby?"

Mrs Havermeyer prepared to clear her throat, but she was too late. "What Ruby was about to say," Mrs Dupont continued, "is that it is time we put you both out of your agony. You might have got away with it in New York, boys, but we are from Vermont."

Tony sighed with equal measures of resignation and relief. "What gave us away?" he asked.

"Many things, young man. Like the way you cross your legs. In Vermont, a lady never reveals her underwear unintentionally. Particularly if the underwear is a pair of boxer shorts."

"And we heard you lift the seat when you went to powder your nose," Mrs Havermeyer added euphemistically.

"Tony, I warned you about that ..." Jack began.

"You should have warned yourself," Mrs Dupont interupted. "Sagging busts on a slim young women are a mite suspicious. When *one* of them sags, it is a dead giveaway."

"Ladies," said Tony, removing his wig with a flourish. "We are at your mercy."

"Oh, we don't blame you a bit," said Mrs Dupont. "When you leave a pairs tournament for a smoke, and come rushing back as if the Big Bad Wolf was after you, and we find out that there were four gangland killings in the parking lot, it isn't difficult to work out why you're leaving New York disguised as *broads*." She enunciated the Brooklinese expression with relish, and leaned forward confidentially. "Admit it, guys. The Mob wants your blood."

Jack thought about going down on his knees, but realised his garter belt might not survive the experience. "You're not going to turn us in?" he pleaded.

"Turn you in? Three days before the Ladies' Teams?" Mrs Dupont was horrified. "We're going to give the two of you a crash course in how to sit, spit, walk, talk and dress. Boys, this is the best chance we've ever had of winning a biggie."

4

By the time they followed their mentors into the Apache-Plaza Hotel, the boys had developed wiggles sassy enough for a Burlesque chorus line. The ill-spent years of gin rummy, poker and bridge were finally paying off. Their arms and legs wouldn't have tempted Fred Astaire to give up Ginger Rogers, but at least they were free of anything resembling a healthy muscle.

Later, from the window of their fourth-floor room, Jack gazed at the beach and savoured the delicious aroma of the sea breeze and Tony's perfume.

"This is the life," he said.

"You don't say," Tony drawled, as he meticulously renewed the lacquer on his false fingernails. "Two days ago the prospect scared you stiff."

"That was before I got the glad eye from two bell hops and that sweet old playboy on the verandah."

"Down, boy! You're getting too wrapped up in the part. Besides, that sweet old playboy is Otis Trilling the Third. No girl is safe with him."

"Tony, in two days as a girl, I've had more passes than in two years as a fellow."

"Well, just you remember you are a fellow, and save your charm for Mrs Dupont. You're playing with her in this evening's Open Pairs."

♦ ♦ ♦ ♦ ♦

Tony was partnering little Mrs Havermeyer. After fifty years of whist and bridge, she was a fair to middling technician, but fifty centuries wouldn't cure her underbidding. Ely Culbertson was spreading it about that, when you sat opposite an underbidder, you should underbid yourself. His theory was that trying to compensate would make her even more cautious.

Tony thought that this was a load of horse feathers. He was looking forward to a bidding orgy, and little Mrs Havermeyer could look forward to long stretches of being dummy.

They started against a pair of stonewallers from Jacksonville. They were old enough to be Tony's grandparents, but stealing tops from them was like taking candy from Shirley Temple's little sister. A baby spade psyche kept them out of a routine game. A jump overcall as weak as a mandarin's tea went unpunished. It was all too easy. Tony thrived on danger, and the event promised to be as exciting as a wet Sunday in Philadelphia.

Then Sugar glided to their table.

The first thing you noticed about a woman might be her hair, her eyes, her lips or her figure, especially if it was shaped like the Coney Island roller-coaster. With Sugar, they all figured in a photo finish.

"Hi!" she said, in a voice like Tennessee honey. Tony was so in love that he almost decided that on the next deal he'd give her an average! "This is my friend Martha, and I'm Sugar. We're just local players. Where are you ladies from?"

At any other time Tony might have taken a tumble to Martha, but with Sugar around she was as anonymous as a nickel in a slot machine. Sugar loved to talk. For her, bridge was something to do with your hands while you made conversation. She said she had taken the game up because it seemed like a good way to meet millionaires, and did they know any one who liked ever-loving blondes and didn't mind if they were short a dozen letters when they recited the alphabet?

North/South Game. Dealer South.

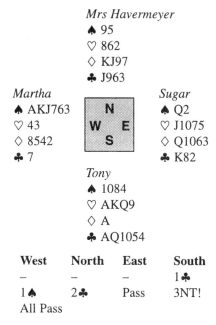

Mrs Havermeyer
♠ 95
♡ 862
◇ KJ97
♣ J963

Martha
♠ AKJ763
♡ 43
◇ 8542
♣ 7

Sugar
♠ Q2
♡ J1075
◇ Q1063
♣ K82

Tony
♠ 1084
♡ AKQ9
◇ A
♣ AQ1054

West	North	East	South
–	–	–	1♣
1♠	2♣	Pass	3NT!
All Pass			

Tony's bid of three no trumps was a monstrosity, even for him. Martha led the ♠K, and Sugar, sitting East declined to contribute her queen. Whether she feared that declarer held four to the ten, or was reluctant to part unnecessarily with an honour, may never be known.

Martha, understandably, switched to a heart. Tony won and, reinforcing the illusion that he had started with ♠Q1084, played a second spade towards dummy's nine. Not unnaturally, this was covered with the jack, and Sugar was forced to win with her queen. She pouted at the sinful waste, and exited with a diamond.

Now all Tony had to do was force out East's ♣K for an easy nine tricks.

"Could we have beaten it?" Sugar asked innocently.

"No," Tony answered her. "I had six certain tricks."

♦ ♦ ♦ ♦ ♦

Jack and Mrs Dupont were doing well when Commodore Van Tromp arrived at their table with the frisky Otis Trilling. They were playing the Van Tromp system, based on sound principles, such as *let the Commodore bid no trumps first.* Otis didn't mind. As dummy, he was free to let his mind wander and his eye rove, and the way it settled on Jack's new bust showed that the old coot wasn't there for the bridge.

"Good evening, Mrs Dupont," he said. "Kindly introduce me to your delectable young partner."

Mrs Dupont wouldn't give Otis the time of day. She didn't even consider him worth a sniff. "Jacqueline," she announced, "this senile delinquent is Otis Trilling the Third, alleged son of Otis Trilling the Second. He has been married eight times, in the futile hope of creating Otis Trilling the Fourth."

Otis was unabashed. "How about it, Jacqueline? Would you like to be the one over the eight?"

Jack didn't reply, but he flashed a bewitching smile in Otis' direction. That should be worth at least an overtrick, he calculated.

"I see you like my face," Otis leered. "You know I had it insured for half a million."

"Really, Mr Trilling? What did you spend the money on?"

Otis smiled till the corners of his mouth threatened to meet at the back of his neck. "Zowee! I think I'm in love."

East/West Game. Dealer South.

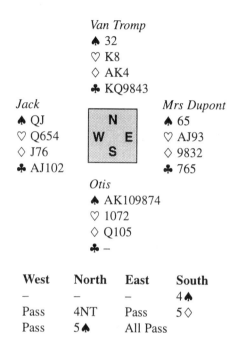

Van Tromp
♠ 32
♡ K8
◇ AK4
♣ KQ9843

Jack
♠ QJ
♡ Q654
◇ J76
♣ AJ102

Mrs Dupont
♠ 65
♡ AJ93
◇ 9832
♣ 765

Otis
♠ AK109874
♡ 1072
◇ Q105
♣ –

West	North	East	South
–	–	–	4♠
Pass	4NT	Pass	5◇
Pass	5♠	All Pass	

The Commodore's four no trump bid was not conventional. He simply wanted to play the contract. Otis had no wish to stop him. His five diamonds was ace-showing, and the Commodore signed off with all guns blazing.

Jack led the ♡4. Dummy played low, and Mrs Dupont won with the ♡J. She considered a trump switch, but for all she knew declarer might have held something like ♠AKQxxxxx ♡xx ◇Qx ♣x. So she cashed the ♡A before switching to a club. When Otis ruffed, Jack 'carelessly' played the ace!

At this point, Otis did something completely out of character. He thought deeply. He laid down the ♠A, noted the fall of West's queen, and thought even more deeply. And he discovered the Theory of Restricted Choice!

And it did him no good whatsoever.

Jack's 'careless' ace of clubs meant that Otis no longer needed to ruff the third heart. He could afford to cater for an unfortunate trump distribution. So he crossed to the ◇ A, threw his last heart on the ♣ K, and called for dummy's spade. He couldn't have put his new theory into words – he just knew that, when West dropped the queen, it had made it more likely that East held the other honour. So he finessed.

Jack took the trick gratefully to defeat a contract when eleven tricks had rolled in at every other table. The Theory would have to wait a few years.

When the brilliancy of Jack's play had dawned on him, Otis' face was a masterpiece of distilled lechery. "Zowee!" he cried. "How would you like to play with me some time?"

"No, thank you, Mr Trilling," said Jack. "I don't care for your single entendres." Glancing at Otis, he realised that the man's previous expression wasn't a masterpiece after all. It was just the first draft of the major work that followed.

"I just love it when you talk dirty," Otis drooled. "How about a diamond bracelet if we finish in the top ninety?"

Jack was shocked. He searched frantically for words to express his womanly outrage, but nothing came. "How many carats?" he enquired serenely.

A little later, Jack and Tony were enjoying a Manhattan in the cocktail lounge, when Sugar joined them.

"Sugar!" Tony rose out of habit. "This is my friend, Jacqueline."

"There's no need to stand up, Antonia," said Sugar.

As Tony sat down, pink with embarrassment, Sugar smiled at Jack. "We've met," she said. "You got two tops, whatever they are. And then I was at the next table when that millionaire, Otis something, asked you to play with him." She looked wistful. "How do you get a millionaire to play with you?" she giggled. "What have you got that I haven't?"

"I could tell you," Jack giggled back. "But you wouldn't believe me."

"Will you join us in a cocktail, Sugar?" Tony intervened smoothly.

"Oh, I'd love to. Especially as there's no men about. One drink and I'm anyone's."

"Really?" said Jack. "Would that be the eleventh or the twelfth?"

"I guess you're joshing me," Sugar smiled winningly. "But you'd better give me a sign, so I know you're doing it. Now tell me how to get partners like Otis Something."

"Well," said Jack. "Looking like you do isn't a bad start. You might cash in on it by memorising their names. And then ...." He squeezed Sugar's knee with an affection that was far from sisterly, until Tony's toe-cap collided painfully with his shin. "I hope you don't mind my telling you, Sugar, but you really should do something about your bridge."

"Do you think so, Jacqueline? Which part of my bridge?"

"Sugar, you sort your hand beautifully. And when the hand is over, you write down the score neatly. Now all you have to do is work on that bit in the middle. Do you recall that three no trumps you played against me?"

North/South Game. Dealer South

```
                    Martha
                    ♠ J43
                    ♡ AK2
                    ◇ K1094
                    ♣ 875
        Jack                        Mrs Dupont
        ♠ KQ1095    ┌─────────┐     ♠ 86
        ♡ J75       │ N       │     ♡ 10983
        ◇ A65       │ W   E   │     ◇ J8
        ♣ Q6        │   S     │     ♣ 109432
                    └─────────┘
                    Sugar
                    ♠ A72
                    ♡ Q64
                    ◇ Q732
                    ♣ AKJ
```

South	West	North	East
1NT	Pass	3NT	All Pass

"I led my king of spades. Quite rightly you took this with the ace. I was sure to hold the queen, so this made dummy's knave a sure third-round winner."

Sugar basked in his praise. "I don't know about, but I do know aces are made to go on kings," she said.

"Right," said Jack. "You crossed to the table with a heart, and played a diamond to your queen. I ducked," he reminded her smugly.

"Yes," she gave a sweet little frown. "I wondered afterwards why you did that."

"I had to duck to preserve my entry, Sugar. Besides, I was sure you would get the suit wrong."

"Pay no attention to Jacqueline's remarks, Sugar," Tony said, starting to fondle the knee which Jack had neglected. "Most players would have placed Mrs Dupont with the ace. I suppose you finessed the diamond ten, and lost to the jack. Now spades were cleared and you were one down. Unlucky."

"Yes, I never seem to get the sweet end of the lollipop."

"If you'll forgive me for saying so, Antonia," Jack purred, "There was a pretty good clue that I held the diamond ace. My partner was a good enough player to rise with it on the first round, and fire through a spade. But tell me, Antonia, darling," he added archly. "You were South. As you're so almighty smart, tell us the masterly line you took."

"I was unlucky to have Ellen Noble as my left-hand opponent."

"Oh really? You poor girl you," Jack waited hopefully for a tale of woe.

"She led the king of spades, like everybody else, and I ducked," Tony said. "Of course she was convinced her partner held the ace, so she continued with the nine of spades, to show she had a diamond entry. I could now afford to play a diamond to the ten safely, but the chances were that East had the jack. I crossed to the king, and advanced dummy's ten. When East's knave appeared, I knew I had ten tricks for a good score."

"That was wonderful, Antonia," said Sugar.

"It was better than that," said Tony. "I decided not to risk the club finesse, and made eleven. An outright top."

"Whatever that is," said Jack sourly.

"You both make it seem so easy," Sugar told them sadly. "I'll never get a millionaire through bridge. I'll just have to try my luck on the beach tomorrow morning."

"A good idea," said Tony. "Which part of the beach?"

5

At least two dozen men were panting hungrily at Sugar as she stretched languidly on the beach. Only Tony ignored her. He had discarded his female disguise in favour of a smart yachting cap and blazer. He sat primly in a deck chair, scanning the Wall Street prices with the casual air of a man who could greet the gain or loss of a few thousand dollars with Olympian indifference.

Sugar was drawn to Tony like a butterfly to a row of sweet peas.

Jack lay on the bed, staring incredulously at the contents of the surprise package from Otis. He recalled gifts from his old flames: gaudy ties, cheap socks, a hand-knitted, knee-length sweater and a five dollar pen which had snapped in two when he savagely recorded a fourteen-hundred point penalty. None of them had given him a tie pin, let alone a diamond bracelet from Tiffany's.

Jack was drawn to Otis like a mouse to a ripe gorgonzola.

"Up twelve," Tony yawned, to nobody in particular.

"I beg your pardon?" said Sugar.

"Oh, I didn't see you there." Tony flicked a grain of sand from his immaculate white flannels. "I was referring to the stock market."

"Is up twelve good?"

"It could be worse. It's usually better to make twenty thousand than to lose it."

Sugar's eyes widened. "You mean you've made twenty gees – I mean thousands, just sitting in that deck chair?"

"You make me sound like a parasite."

"Oh, no. I'm sure you're as American as I am."

"I doubt it. I'm afraid I'm from Boston. My name is Tony, by the way. I can't tell you my second name. I'm here incognito."

"That's nice," she smiled blankly. "I'm Sugar. Sugar ... Dubois. Are you here on vacation?"

"Not exactly, Miss Dubois. I'm trying out my new yacht."

"Oh! Which one is it?"

Tony waved elegantly in the direction of Otis Trilling's sleek ocean-going masterpiece. "That one."

"It's very nice."

"Perhaps you'd care to look over it some time."

"I'd love to. When?"

He produced a diary and pretended to consult it. "I already have a dinner engagement, but why don't we meet here at midnight?"

◆ ◆ ◆ ◆ ◆

Jack had been given the afternoon off to play with Otis in a minor pairs event. He had decided to put off wearing his diamond bracelet until he had a pair of matching ear rings. This was hard on his partner, but a girl had to have principles.

A few greased palms had secured them North-South berths in a cosy corner, where Otis' valet served champagne and canapés. By the seventh board, the old souse was well into his second bottle.

"I was driven to drink by a woman," Otis said, with a reminiscent hiccough. "It is a matter of deep regret that I never properly thanked her."

"Otis, you are definitely a kindred spirit." Jack extended his glass. "Fill her up, pal. My father would turn in his grave if I let anyone outdrink me. I'm afraid he was the town drunk."

"Never mind, Jacqueline." Otis patted Jack's hand. "Being the town drunk is not so bad."

"In New York?"

Their next opponents were Homer and Adelaide, a married couple from Miami. Like all the richer people in the tournament, they were acquaintances of Otis.

"Hello, Otis," said Homer. "I hope you're behaving yourself."

"I know you do, Homer." Otis permitted himself a well-bred belch. "You always were a picklepuss."

East/West Game. Dealer South.

Adelaide
♠ K105
♡ J754
◇ 432
♣ 654

Otis
♠ 9762
♡ 983
◇ QJ108
♣ K7

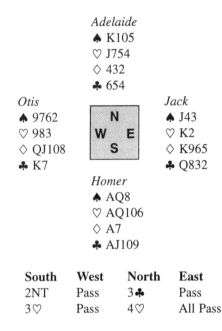

Jack
♠ J43
♡ K2
◇ K965
♣ Q832

Homer
♠ AQ8
♡ AQ106
◇ A7
♣ AJ109

South	West	North	East
2NT	Pass	3♣	Pass
3♡	Pass	4♡	All Pass

Homer was very nearly as good a player as he thought he was, which made him the cat's pyjamas. Adelaide's three clubs was the Boston forerunner to Stayman, and located the four-four fit. Her heart raise was a touching tribute to her husband's card play.

Otis led the ◇ Q. Adelaide put down dummy without a blush. "Thank you, honey," Homer said with all the enthusiasm of a man about to stroke a dead rattlesnake. Then he brightened. With the wind behind him, and including the diamond ruff, he could see nine sure tricks. His sole entry to the table meant he could take the even-money heart finesse for the tenth. But there was a much better line. If he could finagle the defence into taking their ♡ K prematurely, he would gain an extra entry and finesse clubs twice. A seventy-five per-cent chance for a top.

He took the second round of diamonds and smartly flicked the ♡ Q onto the table. Otis played low. So, without batting a mascara-covered eyelid, did Jack. Homer shot a suspicious glance in his direction. He saw a weirdly attractive female, who wasn't short enough for Otis, but sure looked dumb enough. Confident that Otis must have been dealt ♡ Kxx, he continued with a low heart to the jack. The sight of the king appearing from his right didn't exactly make his day, but Homer was nothing if not a fighter. He ruffed Jack's diamond return, and drew the last trump. Then he fired the last shot in his locker – a small spade to the ten.

This was not a success.

"Homer, honey!" his wife protested. "You should have taken the heart finesse."

"You don't say." Homer spoke through clenched teeth. "So I was wrong to reject a fifty-fifty chance in favour of a three-to-one alternative."

"And I object to your finessing the spade ten," Otis offered surprisingly.

"What do you mean? It was my only hope."

"Homer, old sport. If I'd held the jack, I would have inserted it."

"I see." Homer seemed doubtful. "Have you been taking lessons, Otis?"

"Yes." Otis was unabashed. "From the sweet young thing opposite."

Jack started to turn his head to see who Otis was referring to, but stopped just in time. "Flattery will get you everywhere," he said.

Those matching ear rings were as good as his.

6

That evening Jack, playing like a true master, resumed his partnership with Mrs Dupont. She was rock solid, and they won the Ladies' pairs by a street and a half. Tony sat opposite little Mrs Havermeyer: with bidding like his it couldn't be called a partnership. They just made the top ten.

Jack shared a victory cocktail with Mrs Dupont, before joining Otis for a tour of the local hot spots. This left the way clear for Tony to get Sugar aboard the old man's yacht.

Sugar took one look at the starboard salon and clapped her hands like a child of four let loose in a candy store. The caviar was chilled, the champagne was iced, the pheasant was stuffed and her goose was cooked.

It was a roué's paradise.

"Oh, it's like a floating mansion!" she gasped.

Tony gave a modest, old-money shrug. "I suppose it's O.K," he said. "For a bachelor. Would you care for some champagne?"

"Yes please."

"And help yourself to caviar or whatever you fancy. I'm afraid I've given the crew shore leave."

"Really?" She smiled up at him as she accepted her glass. "Does that mean I'm all alone in the ocean with a dangerous man."

"I'm afraid not. I'm not at all dangerous."

"I bet that's what you tell all the girls."

"I mean it." He sat down on the sofa and chewed sadly at a fried chicken leg. "I'm afraid life threw me a dirty curve."

"You poor darling." Sugar sat beside him, oozing sympathy. "Tell me about it."

"I was engaged to be married. We were made for each other. Both from Mayflower families. Both keen on opera, ballet ... bridge."

Sugar brightened. She was beginning to think she and Tony had nothing in common, but one out of four wasn't bad. "I didn't know you played bridge," she said.

"I don't." He let out a melancholy sigh. "I gave it up when she died. We were crossing Fifth Avenue, puzzling over a problem in the *New York Times*. Then, halfway across the street, she stopped in her tracks. 'I've got the answer!' she cried. 'You should play the ....' " He broke off, his voice shaking. "I've never found out what I should have played. She was hit by a two-ton truck."

"That's terrible."

"Since that day, women have left me cold. And whenever I try to play bridge, all I can see is that fateful deal in the *Times*. And every time I look at that fateful deal, all I can see is her tiny foot, peeping out from under the truck. I've been to all the top psychiatrists. Some say I'll never solve that bridge problem until I've ... made it with a girl. Some say I'll never make it with a girl until I've solved the problem."

"And what do you say?"

"I don't know what to say."

"Well, would you like me to take a shot at your other little problem?"

"It'll be a waste of time, I'm afraid." He shrugged his shoulders. "But I suppose there's no harm in trying."

She began to stroke the back of his neck, and plant butterfly kisses all over his face. By the time she reached his lips, he was starting to melt. He didn't move a muscle, but when the kiss finished, he was so in love he felt like calling for a clergyman.

Sugar had never been so thrilled. Every man she'd known had come on so strong, she'd felt as if she was fighting off a sex-starved octopus. Tony's complete lack of response was the biggest turn-on of her sweet young life. She waited breathlessly for his reaction.

"Would you like to see the deal?"

"Yes please. I would." She choked back her disappointment. "I'm not much good, but people say I'm very lucky."

He presented her with a press cutting.

Love All Dealer South.

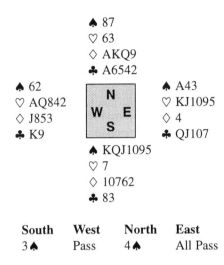

♠ 87
♡ 63
◇ AKQ9
♣ A6542

♠ 62
♡ AQ842
◇ J853
♣ K9

♠ A43
♡ KJ1095
◇ 4
♣ QJ107

♠ KQJ1095
♡ 7
◇ 10762
♣ 83

South	West	North	East
3♠	Pass	4♠	All Pass

"The problem is to make four spades against the best defence," said Tony.

"Well you tell me what the best defence is," Sugar said cheerfully. "Then we'll figure out how to beat it."

"Deciding the best defence is part of the puzzle. We're given that West leads a trump. Now imagine that you're East. What do you play?"

"I take with my ace."

"Seems like a good play to me," Tony lied smoothly. "The trouble is..." He nibbled delicately at a plump pheasant. "When declarer gets in he'll now make five spades, four diamonds, and the ace of clubs."

Sugar thought deeply. Two glasses of champagne later, she saw the light. "Then suppose I don't take with the ace of trumps?"

Tony did a creditable impression of Rodin's Thinker. "I think you're on to something," he told her. "You win the *second* trump and switch to a diamond. This maintains the threat of a diamond ruff, because declarer won't be able to get to hand to draw the last trump. That's very clever of you, Sugar."

"Does this mean we've solved it?"

"Not quite, my dear. Declarer may find a counter. After the first trump, he might switch to ..."

Sugar leapt in. "Clubs? Diamonds?" Tony shook his head doubtfully. "Or maybe a heart," she added brightly.

"That's it!" he said. "A scissors coup, breaking communications between defenders and killing the diamond ruff. Sugar, you certainly know some advanced plays."

"Beginner's luck, I guess. Is that it?"

"Not yet. I've just realised that an alert defence will continue hearts."

"Is that bad?"

"It could be," he said. "If declarer were to ruff that heart and continue with a spade, he still couldn't get to hand to draw the last trump."

"Oh!" She looked disappointed and bit her lip in a desperate effort of concentration. "So I guess he'd better not ruff that heart."

Tony's eyes widened in amazement. "Sugar, that's amazing! If he were to discard something ..."

"A diamond?" she suggested. "Or a club?" she amended, seeing his dubious expression.

"Of course," he said. "Now he can return to hand by ruffing a club. Sugar, you've found the best defence and the best declarer play. And you've made four spades."

"It was nothing," she said. "You helped."

"No, it was all you. I didn't think anyone so beautiful would be so intelligent."

She slid along the sofa, moving close to him. "Does that mean you're cured?"

"It's too early to say." He casually draped his arm behind her, along the back of the sofa, ready to move in for the kill. "You've helped me beat the *New York Times*. I'm sure that I can now play bridge again. The question is …."

He paused, trying to look shy. This wasn't easy for a guy who'd seen more sex than a policeman's torch. "Do you think you could check whether my other problem has cleared up?"

"Perhaps you'd like to see for yourself," she said breathlessly, "but promise me you won't put up the best defence."

The Dupont quartet were lying equal second in the Ladies' Teams. In the final round they were up against the tournament leaders. Jack reckoned that they would need two game swings for a good shot at the trophy.

The opposition was tough, but he felt good as he sorted his first hand. He had a sound one no trump opening. His diamond bracelet with the matching earrings were the envy of the field. Otis Trilling was kibitzing with an expression of dog-like devotion. What more could a gal want?

Love All. Dealer South.

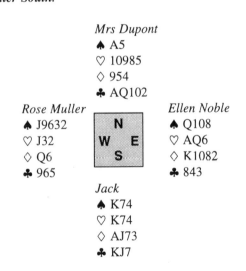

Mrs Dupont
♠ A5
♡ 10985
♢ 954
♣ AQ102

Rose Muller
♠ J9632
♡ J32
♢ Q6
♣ 965

Ellen Noble
♠ Q108
♡ AQ6
♢ K1082
♣ 843

Jack
♠ K74
♡ K74
♢ AJ73
♣ KJ7

West	North	East	South
–	–	–	1NT
Pass	2♣	Pass	2♢
Pass	3NT	All Pass	

The play was Byzantine. Spades were led and continued. Jack won the second round. He then confidently advanced dummy's ♡10.

Reading the situation in a flash, Ellen Noble correctly contributed her ♡Q. Jack, determined to deprive Muller of an entry, played low. Realising that a third spade would now be futile, Noble switched smartly to the ♢10, hoping to scoop up declarer's knave.

Jack countered by rising with the ♢A. He crossed to a club and played a second round of hearts. Noble played low without a flicker, but Jack rose with his ♡K, and a third round felled both outstanding honours.

In theory, the defence had five winners. In practice, they couldn't cash them. Jack was home with two spades, two hearts, a diamond and four clubs.

"Well played," said Ellen Noble, scenting an adverse swing.

"Well defended," said Jack, holding out his champagne glass for Otis to fill.

Several flat boards followed. Tony was getting desperate. Then he was given a chance to bring off a typically spectacular deception. But the risk was breathtaking.

Game All. Dealer South.

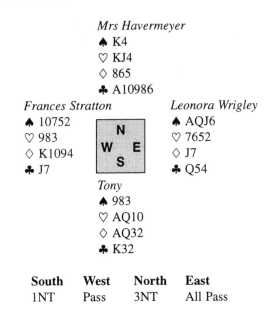

Mrs Havermeyer
♠ K4
♡ KJ4
◇ 865
♣ A10986

Frances Stratton
♠ 10752
♡ 983
◇ K1094
♣ J7

Leonora Wrigley
♠ AQJ6
♡ 7652
◇ J7
♣ Q54

Tony
♠ 983
♡ AQ10
◇ AQ32
♣ K32

South	West	North	East
1NT	Pass	3NT	All Pass

At the other table, Rose Muller had taken the obvious line of winning the heart lead in hand, and ducking a club to East. Jack returned the ◇ J, Muller finessed, and the marked spade switch set the contract by two tricks.

Against Tony, Frances Stratton also chose to lead a top of nothing heart, and Tony assessed the merits of the routine line. Then he considered his opponents, the tournament leaders, the title holders, both sharp performers. They were good enough to fall for a classic con. Besides, routine lines were never written up in *The Bridge World*. So he won the first trick on the table and ran the ♣ 10 to West's Jack.

Frances Stratton could have written a book on avoidance plays. It was obvious that declarer was protecting a weakness in her own hand, and she had a shrewd idea where that weakness was. Suppressing a smile, she led a low diamond ....

Mrs Dupont had won her first biggie.

Celebrations were gay, but brief. Now that Jack and Tony were in the big time, they had to be wary of questions about the bridge background they didn't have. Besides, Tony had a date by the pier with Sugar, and Jack had to change into something that would show off the necklace Otis had promised him.

Just before they left, Mrs Dupont casually gave Jack a bulky envelope. "Put it away," she said. "It's a nice little bonus for the two of you. You both played like angels."

"Thank you," Jack replied. "And you, ladies. You were both terrific."

"But you're professionals," said Mrs Havermeyer. "We're only amateurs."

"You mind what you're saying," Mrs Dupont reproved her. "Amateurs built the Ark. Professionals built the Titanic."

The men made their excuses, and took the elevator to their floor.

And then a noxious substance hit the fan.

7

Spats Coleano looked around the Apache Plaza, and found it good. He was down for the annual conference of the Friends of Italian Pasta. Like every leading member of the Syndicate, Spats owned a spaghetti joint or two, so the conference title was no lie, although it would do until a lie came along.

The hotel was also hosting a bridge event. The whole country was caught up in the bridge craze. And where there was a craze there was scratch. He'd have to find out if the game needed organising.

Spats seemed to recall that he'd had that thought before. Yes, it was on the night he rubbed out Big Vinny. He frowned at the memory. It may have been a mistake. Big Vinny had been an old friend of Little Napoleon. And Little Napoleon was Numero Uno in the Syndicate.

Another mistake had been letting the two witnesses off the hook. But they were bridge pros – they were bound to show up. Maybe at this very tournament.

Spats stepped into the elevator, closely shadowed by Danny the Ox and Fingers Flannery. He took off his hat when he saw there were two broads present. There was something vaguely familiar about them, and they seemed nervous. He could almost hear their knees knocking. But he guessed that the sight of Danny the Ox grinning like a baboon on heat would make Jack Dempsey nervous.

The lift stopped at Spats' floor and he got out. He gave the two nervous broads a long, hard look, and came to a decision. He'd have to make some enquiries about them.

◆ ◆ ◆ ◆ ◆

Only one thing stopped Jack from smashing the world record for packing a suitcase – Tony was even faster.

"If I sell my new jewellery we can live for ten years in South America," said Jack.

"What on? Bananas?"

"Well at least we'd *live*. Did you see that look he gave us?"

"See it? I *felt* it!" Tony clenched his teeth to stop them chattering. He opened the door an inch and peered out. "We'll leave by the elevator," he said. "Lightning won't strike twice in the same place."

Wrong! The elevator stopped at the floor below, and Spats got in, followed by Danny and Fingers. They were on their way to join the Friends of Italian Pasta.

"What a nice surprise!" Spats smiled. He thrust himself between the elevator boy and his controls. One piercing glance stifled the boy's protests, and the cold eyes returned to Jack and Tony.

Fear always sent Tony's imagination into double time. He remembered a movie about two Russian aristocrats fleeing from the Red Guards. Whenever one came near, they engaged in a casual conversation about Dostoievsky. This convinced the soldier that they had nothing to fear. Spats' interest in Dostoievsky was probably limited, but he was a curly wolf at bridge.

"Tell me, Jacqueline," said Tony, in his most melodious contralto. "In the last round but one, how did you beat three no trumps on board twelve?" He produced a pencilled record of the deal. It was one he was saving for his memoirs.

North/South Game. Dealer South.

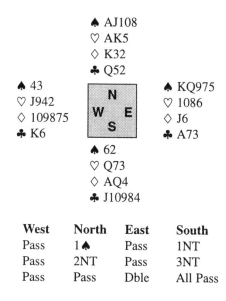

♠ AJ108
♡ AK5
◇ K32
♣ Q52

♠ 43
♡ J942
◇ 109875
♣ K6

♠ KQ975
♡ 1086
◇ J6
♣ A73

♠ 62
♡ Q73
◇ AQ4
♣ J10984

West	North	East	South
Pass	1♠	Pass	1NT
Pass	2NT	Pass	3NT
Pass	Pass	Dble	All Pass

"Board twelve ..." Jack, catching on quickly, appeared to scan his memory. "Oh yes. I was East," he said. "In view of my double, Mrs Dupont led her top spade. Declarer called for dummy's ten, and I ducked."

"That was a very good shot."

"I must admit I thought so too, Antonia. She played on clubs, partner came in with the king, and led another spade. Declarer played the jack, I won and cleared the suit. In with the ace of clubs, I cashed two more spades to hold her to eight tricks. How did you make it, dear? Did East forget to duck?"

"I didn't give her the chance." Tony said proudly. "On the spade lead, *I* played dummy's *eight*."

"You clever little devil, you. Now the defence is right up a gum tree."

Spats had been peering over Tony's shoulder to follow the play. "My compliments, ma'am," he said. "The play of the spade eight was worthy of the hottest pros in the game. I knew a couple in New York who were that great. But they disappeared a few days back. Perhaps you heard of them? Citrus and Melon?"

The two hot pros were out of the elevator and down the stairs before Spats could blink. He should have remembered their lightning dash from the McKinley car lot. Danny and Fingers lumbered after them, but without their machine guns they were never a serious threat.

They crouched in the third floor linen closet and struggled to get their breath back. Jack went through his purse. He still had their money and his jewellery. Things could be worse.

Tony wasn't so sure." We shouldn't have stopped here," he said. "We were twenty lengths ahead of those two torpedoes. We could have made it out of the hotel with no trouble at all. It's my fault – for listening to you."

"That's right. Blame your partner as usual," Jack scolded. "Suppose Spats had gone down in the elevator. He would have been in the lobby a minute before us, waiting to pick us off. You should listen to Mrs Dupont. Two bites at the cherry are often best."

"Well, genius, when do we take our second bite?"

"We'll give it ten minutes, then go down by the stairs. He may have given up by then."

"And if he hasn't?"

Jack gave him the withering look of a man who has calculated every last detail. "We'll improvise."

Spats had taken a lift to the lobby as soon as the witnesses had escaped. Now he and his two gorillas hid behind three pillars, to form an infernal triangle, scanning the departing guests for signs of bridge pros in disguise. They could still be dressed as broads. Or maybe they'd changed back into guys. It didn't matter. In either case Spats would get them.

Five minutes passed. Ten. It would soon be time for the pasta conference, and Little Napoleon was known to be somewhat bigoted about late-comers.

Then he became aware of two female heads, peering round the pillar at the foot of the staircase. He motioned Danny and Fingers to keep still. Soon the two heads were followed by two female bodies, which began to sneak across the lobby towards the main doors of the Apache Plaza.

Spats strolled casually towards them, while, at a snap of his fingers, his two henchmen joined him to converge on their quaking targets. But, with an inspiration born of fear, Tony seized two nearby suitcases and hurled them like a pro, straight to the knees of Danny and Fingers. Then he and Jack disappeared round a corner and through the first door they came to. The room was arranged for a formal banquet, and they dived under a table to hide behind the long linen table-cloth.

Meanwhile, Spats gazed down at the sad baffled faces of Danny the Ox and Fingers Flannery. Maybe he should rub *them* out and recruit the two bridge pros. But that would have to wait, for the delegates were beginning to file into the Conference.

Tony and Jack were just about to leave their latest hiding place, when the sound of fifty pairs of heavy feet told him that the room was about to fill up. The Friends of Italian Pasta were about to confer.

And to prove it, as three pairs of feet appeared in front of Jack and Tony, they saw that the middle pair was wearing immaculate white spats.

A loud cheer from the delegates signalled the arrival of Little Napoleon. He held up his hands and, after a show of reluctance, the applause stopped.

"Fellow pasta lovers," he said. "Ten years ago, I was democratically elected president of this organisation. And I believe I made a wise choice.

When I took over, we were as broke as the Ten Commandments. Last year we made a hundred and twenty million before taxes and a hundred and twenty million after taxes." The gale of laughter reflected not so much the intelligence of his audience as the fact that they had heard the joke nine times before.

"Of course we had our disagreements." He glanced in Spats' direction. "The death of Big Vinnie from acute lead poisoning was a sad loss."

Every pair of eyes in the room turned towards Spats, who looked impassively back at the President.

"Some say that our friend from New York is getting too big for his spats," Little Napoleon continued. "But I say that a little ambition is no bad thing. I hear that our friend is thinking of taking over bridge. Perhaps he thinks that this will help find those two bridge pros who escaped from him. Well, we in the organisation believe in helping our friends. So here for Spats is a nice grand slam bonus, which I know he'll appreciate."

A huge iced cake was wheeled in, while Little Napoleon conducted a spontaneous rendering of *He's a Jolly Good Fellow*. This gave Spats a very un-jolly feeling indeed, but he sat there transfixed. Then a gunman's head appeared through the icing, and once again Jack and Tony heard the terrifying rattle of machine gun bullets meting out their awesome justice.

As the gunman disappeared and the three bodies slid to the floor beside them, Jack and Tony made their third rapid exit of the evening.

"Somebody grab those dames!" screamed Little Napoleon, but he was too late. FBI agents, who were keeping an eye on the Pasta gang, had heard the noise and were coming in to investigate.

In thirty seconds, the boys were in front of the hotel, where Otis was waiting patiently in his open convertible.

"Otis, this is Antonia," Jack said, as they leapt into their seats. "Take us to your motor boat and make it fast! The mob's after us."

"Zowee!" said Otis, and grinned with boyish delight as he drove off. In two minutes they reached the pier, where Sugar waited anxiously.

"Otis, meet Sugar," said Jack abruptly. "She's Antonia's girl," he added, irritated at the attention his beau was paying to Sugar.

"Pleased to meet you," said Otis. "And don't worry, I'm very broad minded. Zowee!"

Sugar sat in the back of the motor boat with Tony. She looked bewildered and vulnerable, until Tony kissed her passionately.

"Tony!" she cried. "You're a cross-dresser."

"Actually, my darling, there's a lot you don't know about me," he said, and began to whisper in her ear.

"Are your friends joining us?" Otis asked Jack.

"I thought the four of us might sail gaily along the coast," said Jack airily, "and possibly steal a few bridge prizes."

"A good idea, my dear. And will they be staying on for the honeymoon?"

"I'm glad you mentioned that, Otis. The truth is I don't think we should get married."

"Why not?"

"I snore terribly."

"I can wear earplugs."

"In the second place, you play the Official System. I'm strictly Culbertson."

"I can change."

"Another thing. I'm a terrible partner. In six months I'll drive you to suicide."

"I'll put up with you. We'll win every event in the mixed calendar".

"Otis." Jack was desperate, he pulled off his wig. "I'm a guy. We won't be able to play in the mixed pairs."

Otis yawned politely. "That's OK. We'll just have to concentrate on the Men's."

2

FRANKENSTEIN'S BRIDGE PARTNER

Fond of you all though I am, I must say that you Earth people are an odd lot. When, over a period of a few months, five men and a woman, all active in the same field, disappear in suspicious circumstances, the media (or even, at the top of their form, the police) might be expected to notice the coincidence. One can even envisage the orgies of alliteration in the tabloid headlines: "Vicars Vexed by Vanishing Vergers" or "Motorists Mourn Missing Mechanics."

The six people in question, however, were only bridge players, so their departures were largely unnoticed.

Which is why I chose them.

According to my preliminary studies of terrestrial trivia, that charming but insignificant geographical area known as the United Kingdom boasted (if that is the right word) more than a million bridge players, yet even their greatest achievements were mentioned only in perfunctory footnotes to the bridge columns.

I found several reasons for the game's failure to appeal to outsiders. One was the strange behaviour of the insiders. For example, when two expert met, instead of opening the conversation with rituals such as "hello" or "I like your new tie," they recited esoteric formulae, like, "You hold ace-queen to five, stiff queen, void ..."

But I digress. In the unlikely event of your visiting my home world, you will find that digression is a planetary idiosyncrasy (which may account for my excessive use of brackets). It suffced for my purpose that bridge, for whatever reasons, held as much media value as yesterday's weather forecast.

And what precisely was my purpose? A good question. Well, I was working for my Doctorate in Omfoozling. (The Earth equivalent, albeit an elementary one, would be biological engineering.) Where I come from, omfoozling, among the higher vertebrates, is a crime punishable by severe nurdling, which is why I came to Earth.

My thesis was (and I quote), "that six carefully selected beings of any given occupation could be omfoozled to create a single entity who, by virtue of possessing the principal talent of each, would become pre-eminent in that occupation."

And if you think that is easy, you have never omfoozled.

I suppose I should introduce myself, but my name cannot be expressed adequately in your limited language. So instead I shall introduce you to my first disappearing bridge player. We shall call him Ivor, for he represented a small UK sub-division, full of short mountains and long faces. I watched him play in a match against Northern Ireland, and soon had the opportunity to admire his considerable skill.

Love All. Dealer North.

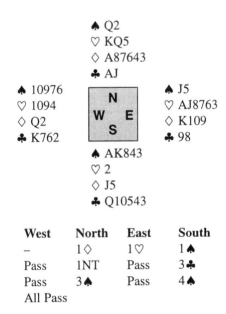

	♠ Q2	
	♡ KQ5	
	◇ A87643	
	♣ AJ	

```
        ♠ Q2
        ♡ KQ5
        ◇ A87643
        ♣ AJ
♠ 10976      N       ♠ J5
♡ 1094    W     E    ♡ AJ8763
◇ Q2         S       ◇ K109
♣ K762               ♣ 98
        ♠ AK843
        ♡ 2
        ◇ J5
        ♣ Q10543
```

West	North	East	South
–	1◇	1♡	1♠
Pass	1NT	Pass	3♣
Pass	3♠	Pass	4♠
All Pass			

The match report will tell you that, in the other room, East won the heart lead and returned the suit. The Irish declarer realising that the contract depended on retaining trump control, banked on a time-honoured principle – establish your side suit first. He called for the the ♣A, followed by the ♣J. The inevitable third round round of the suit was ruffed by East, and West's fourth trump eventually set the contract.

Ivor banked on the same principle, but added the first of the qualities I was looking for – technique. In dummy with the second heart, he advanced the ♣J! The Irish West took the trick and returned a heart. This forced Ivor to ruff, but the rest of the hand was child's play. The intrepid Welshman crossed to the ♣A, drew three rounds of trumps and ran his club winners. The defence could only make their trump trick once and, with a faint smile, reminiscent of Steve McQueen in *The Cincinnati Kid,* Ivor claimed the rest.

Finding the winning line may not be difficult as a problem, but to spot it at the table is the hallmark of the expert technician. To some extent, technique can be learned from books or by experience. However, as there are an infinite number of possible situations (I have counted them) it would require an infinite amount of study to learn the appropriate techniques for each. And yours is a short-lived race.

After the session, the Welsh went to the bar for a quaint custom called a post-mortem. This is a contest where each player claims credit for his side's successes, and blames its disasters on his team-mates. Winning the post-mortem is often considered more important than winning the match.

Interrupting one of these contests is not normally conducive to long life, but it was a simple matter to get Ivor to myself. When I appeared beside him, he saw an impossibly lovely girl, with a forty-inch bust and a twenty-two-inch waist. To avoid a stampede, I projected myself to his colleagues with the two measurements exactly reversed. (A simple trick if you know how. You've probably seen it in *Star Trek*.)

"I loved the way you played that four spades," I said.

"Did you honestly?" Ivor blushed boyishly.

"I'd heard how good you were," I said, "but I had to come and see for myself."

"Really?" he gaped. "You mean you came here just to see me?"

"Yes, and when you played that jack of clubs, I knew my journey hadn't been wasted. Do you do everything as well as you play the dummy?"

"Well, I don't know about that," he stammered.

"I'd like to find out," I said, opting for a subtle approach. "Your room or mine?"

As we went upstairs, I marvelled at the gullibility of the human male, who, even when he had a spotty face, dandruff and the belly of an over-the-hill sumo wrestler, could be made to believe he was sexually irresistible. No other creature in the galaxy is so naive, though the Aldabaranian munchwardler comes close.

Ivor, like many male bridge addicts, liked to talk about bridge deals before, after and during the sex act. (Female addicts just think about bridge deals.)

"Where did you acquire your superb technique?" I asked him.

He stopped what he was doing and thought for a moment. "I learned it from a cute little blonde number called Blodwyn, in Merthyr Tydfil."

I pricked up my ears, but managed to restore them to their original shape before he noticed. "She must have been a marvellous player," I remarked casually, sensing that Blodwyn might be another candidate for the omfoozle.

He seemed puzzled. "Oh, you mean my bridge technique." He gave an embarrassed little laugh. "I suppose it just comes naturally."

"You don't read books?" I asked.

"I used to," he said. "Now I just glance at the odd column."

I decided to test him with one of Hugh Kelsey's lesser-known classics. "You hold..." I began.

East/West Game. Dealer South.

♠ 10532
♥ A
♦ J106
♣ AQJ107

♠ AQJ4
♥ 983
♦ AQ4
♣ K82

West	North	East	South
–	–	–	1♠
Pass	3♣	Pass	4♣
Pass	4♠	Pass	5♦
Pass	5♥	Pass	6♠
All Pass			

Lead: ♥Q

He pondered for less than a minute. "Well," he said, "if trumps are three-two, it's a piece of cake, isn't it? And if they're five-nil, there's no hope whatsoever."

"So we need to concentrate on the four-one breaks," I interpolated helpfully.

"Of course." He gave me a patronising peck, and slowed down to allow for my limited intellect. "I will lead the ten of spades from dummy."

"East plays the king," I said.

"Then I duck." He paused to let the significance of that play sink in. "Now I won't need the diamond finesse, because I can ruff two hearts in dummy."

"But suppose West has the spade king," I said.

"Then it's a little more awkward," he conceded. "His best defence is to hold up till the second round. Now after a third trump is led, I shall need the diamond finesse."

This was a model answer, and undoubtedly his own, for although not a telepath, I am highly sensitive to emotions. The dear little Celt was telling the truth; the deal had been new to him. He was a natural; I needed to look no further for my first "volunteer".

You would probably attribute Ivor's ability to solve difficult and original problems to spatial intelligence. An omfoozler who knows his business can separate this into seven categories, and Ivor certainly had the one I wanted.

In case you are wondering why such a divine declarer had not achieved world renown, I should explain that, after playing one hand like an angel, he was quite capable of flooring a stone-cold contract on the very next board. And as for his bidding...

Ivor and I were betrothed before breakfast. As he proudly announced his engagement to a 22-40-44 woman, five Welsh mouths fell open as one. When I explained that I was a millionairess with a weakness for impoverished bridge pros, my popularity increased so dramatically that I thought I was projecting the wrong vital statistics.

A few days later, we left for a world tour of indefinite length.

My second target was Josephine, a lady with a waspish tongue, a basilisk eye and a list of psychologically battered ex-partners long enough to fill a small telephone directory. She acknowledged her shortcomings; she even sought professional help. After six months of therapy, her analyst advised her to take up solitaire.

I met Josephine at a fashionable London club, where I watched her play a session of high-stake partnership rubber bridge. Her partner was Deirdre, an English international who made no secret of the fact. By agreement, both pairs were using a modest range of conventions.

Game All. Dealer South.

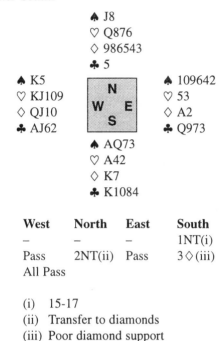

```
                    ♠ J8
                    ♡ Q876
                    ◇ 986543
                    ♣ 5
    ♠ K5              N          ♠ 109642
    ♡ KJ109                      ♡ 53
    ◇ QJ10        W     E        ◇ A2
    ♣ AJ62           S           ♣ Q973
                    ♠ AQ73
                    ♡ A42
                    ◇ K7
                    ♣ K1084
```

West	North	East	South
–	–	–	1NT(i)
Pass	2NT(ii)	Pass	3◇(iii)
All Pass			

(i)   15-17
(ii)   Transfer to diamonds
(iii) Poor diamond support

Sitting East, Josephine won the diamond lead, and switched to a spade. Declarer played low. Deirdre took with her ♠K, and considered her next action with a distinct absence of enthusiasm. A fine defender when sitting opposite a human being, she could infer enough about the distribution to suspect that every choice seemed to have a drawback. If she cashed the ♣A, for example, declarer would surely have time to discard all dummy's heart losers on his black suit winners. Yet, if she didn't cash it, declarer would not lose a club.

Without much hope, she chose a deceptive ♡9. Declarer won on the table, cashed the ♠J, crossed to his ◇K, and advanced the ♠A. Deirdre's agony was renewed. Reluctantly, she ruffed with her winning trump, but this meant that dummy's losing club disappeared.

Deirdre, who was herself a redoubtable mixer, adopted her usual post-mortem strategy when playing with Josephine. She retaliated first. "Your spade switch at trick two was not exactly a success," she observed.

"No," Josephine gave her a smile of undiluted acidity. "Guesswork is not my strong point, Deirdre, any more than card play is yours."

"How sweet of you to point that out," Deirdre hissed. "And where exactly did I go wrong?"

"I think it was your decision to take up the game," said Josephine, after a few moments' thought. "Oh, you mean on *this* deal! It was your puerile heart switch at trick three."

"What do you mean, puerile?"

"Juvenile, childish, infantile. I'm sure you've heard the word many times before. A responsible adult would have switched to the *king* of hearts."

Deirdre was quick enough to see that this would have set the contract, but was not ready to admit defeat. "Double dummy!" she snapped.

"Of course." Josephine's response was withering. "By that time you should have known the location of every card."

She was exaggerating, of course. Moreover, she was not a top-class defender, and would probably never have found the right switch herself. Which made her even more infuriating. But you can see that the king of hearts is a killing return. It removes one of declarer's entries for the long spade, and ensures that the defence eventually makes two heart tricks.

Realising this, Deirdre decided to lose gracefully. "All right, Josephine. I'll let you have the last word."

"Thank you, darling." Josephine smiled seraphically. "Zythum."

Believe it or not, I had just witnessed Josephine in a benevolent mood. At the top of her form, she could generate a torrent of abuse which engulfed partner, opponents and spectators alike. And she got away with it, as most of her victims were too terrified to fight back. A foolhardy man called Horace once asked her whether she intended to teach the whole club everything she knew. Her reply, "I'll teach them everything we both know, Horace. It won't take any longer," was worthy of Bette Davis in *All About Eve*, I thought.

Josephine's mordant wit was not my object, however; in fact, all her disagreeable traits would have to be ruthlessly eliminated. They were merely the dark side of what I coveted – her irresistible will to win. But I'm sure you've guessed that. Her very presence put the fear of God into her enemies. As the *Bridge Players' Encyclopaedia* puts it, she had the gift of making opponents feel they were facing someone of a higher order. She was the ultimate competitor; she was awesome; she was *Lethal Weapon Nine.*

Both sides had a partscore when she found herself in a tricky two no trump contract to clinch the rubber.

Game All. Dealer West.

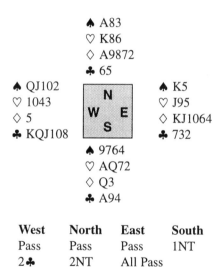

	♠ A83	
	♡ K86	
	◇ A9872	
	♣ 65	

♠ QJ102		♠ K5
♡ 1043		♡ J95
◇ 5		◇ KJ1064
♣ KQJ108		♣ 732

	♠ 9764	
	♡ AQ72	
	◇ Q3	
	♣ A94	

West	North	East	South
Pass	Pass	Pass	1NT
2♣	2NT	All Pass	

Clubs were led and continued, Josephine winning the third round. The obvious line of crossing to the ♡K and venturing a diamond towards the queen was not a good idea. East would surely rise with the king and switch to a spade, knocking out dummy's entry for the long diamonds.

Like the Starship Enterprise, Josephine decided to boldly go where nobody else would be seen dead. Radiating self-confidence, she led a spade towards the table, willing her opponent to believe that this was her strong suit.

It worked. West inserted the ♠10, and East failed to unblock his king under the ace. Now a diamond towards the queen ensured eight tricks.

Yes, I realise that the defence was witless – I can imagine your incredulous gasp as I described it – but Josephine had the Indian sign on both defenders. Against anyone less intimidating, West might have inserted the ♠Q, to make the position clear. And yes, I agree that East should have unblocked anyway, but there is no harm in making things easy for partner, is there?

Are you dazzled by Josephine's barefaced cheek, or have you spotted a play she missed? Technically, declarer's best chance, against good defenders, is to cash four rounds of hearts and run the ◇Q. East can later be endplayed for the eighth trick (as long as declarer reads the position accurately).

"Superbly played," I exaggerated, my voice virile and vibrant.

She turned, to see a man who packed the style of Cary Grant and the youthful charm of Tom Cruise into the body of Arnold Schwarznegger. (My meticulous study of Earth films was proving invaluable.) The pupils of her eyes dilated with passion, but she was speechless for once.

"We must play together some time," I said, revealing an impossibly perfect set of teeth.

"Yes, we must." She smiled back at me, revealing six fillings and a rather lop-sided crown.

"I believe the session is over," I said, dimpling cutely. "I think I'll go for a drink."

"What a coincidence," she prevaricated, and the other players gaped at the sight of her leaving with a man who packed the suave sophistication of the Three Stooges into the body of Charles Laughton in *The Hunchback of Notre Dame*. We soon had the bar to ourselves.

We sipped Chardonnay, and I gazed hungrily into her eyes, like Anthony Hopkins in *The Silence of the Lambs*.

"I want to be your next partner," I announced vibrantly.

"Why?" She had enough self-awareness to be amazed.

"I'm a masochist," I grinned boyishly. "I love your trenchant wit, your caustic charm. To others, they may be terrifying. To me, they're thrilling – almost an aphrodisiac. Besides," I added for good measure. "I shall never become your victim. My bridge is faultless."

She gushed girlishly. "The moment I saw you, I knew we had something in common."

We dined at Le Gavroche, and slept at the Ritz. She proposed to me over breakfast at the Connaught; I accepted over lunch at Maxime's, Paris. She wrote to her friends, predicting that she would be away for weeks – a chronological understatement.

I was pleased with Josephine. No longer would she bite her opponents' ears off. I would transform her into a Rocky Marciano, the nice guy who never finished second. Besides, I needed a female for the omfoozle, in order to demonstrate my ability to handle cross-sexual complications.

Thanks to some barbaric contributions from both sides of the Atlantic, the English language has become a triumph of the picturesque over the precise. I am not accusing you all of speaking like Al Pacino in *Scarface*, or Al Doolittle in *My Fair Lady*, but you do tend to misuse even simple words like "imagination."

Imagine (if you'll pardon the expression) a fine player putting up a routine defence against a contract which appears to be "on ice." (Yet another confusing epithet. Why, if "making" a cold woman is impossible, should making a cold contract be inevitable?) Declarer sails home, but, with that kindness and consideration typical of bridge players everywhere, he points out that an alternative line would have sunk him. The fine player's lapse is put down to a lack of imagination.

This is patently absurd: the fine player was just bone-idle. Great defenders do not rely on divine inspiration, like Ben Kingsley in *Ghandi*. The business of breaking the unbreakable is not for the feeble or the faint-hearted. Technique is not always enough. Sometimes a myriad of lines

must be evaluated in the often futile quest for one which offers a faint ray
of hope. This does not call for imagination, or inspiration; it requires
perspiration, like Spencer Tracy in *Edison the Man.*

Oliver, the third potential member of my sextet, was a case in point. In his
pomp, he could produce prodigious bursts of energy from an apparently
inexhaustible well. He was like Alec Guinness in *Star Wars*: the force was
with him. (Though it deserted him shamelessly during many of his bidding
sequences.)

By now, he had become the world's oldest active bridge star. Yet only a
few years previously, he had given us this masterwork:

East/West Game. Dealer South.

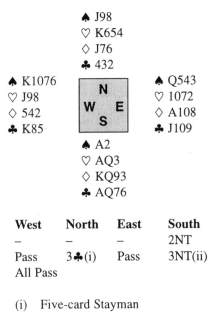

```
                    ♠ J98
                    ♡ K654
                    ◇ J76
                    ♣ 432
    ♠ K1076         ┌─────────┐         ♠ Q543
    ♡ J98           │    N    │         ♡ 1072
    ◇ 542           │  W   E  │         ◇ A108
    ♣ K85           │    S    │         ♣ J109
                    └─────────┘
                    ♠ A2
                    ♡ AQ3
                    ◇ KQ93
                    ♣ AQ76
```

West	North	East	South
–	–	–	2NT
Pass	3♣(i)	Pass	3NT(ii)
All Pass			

(i)   Five-card Stayman
(ii) 2-3 or 2-2 in the majors

On lead against a confidently bid 3NT, Oliver decided to open with a spade.
The only question was which spade? The six would have been routine. The
ten would have attracted most of the smart money, hoping to find
something like ♠A9 doubleton in declarer's hand and ♠Jxx in dummy.

Oliver selected the ♠K, an inferior choice only when declarer held ♠AQ doubleton opposite three or four to the knave. Taking in hand, declarer played a diamond to the knave and ace. East switched to the ♣J, and it seemed harmless to finesse.

In with the ♣K, Oliver artlessly advanced the ♠6. Not one to be caught napping, declarer went up with dummy's ♠J, and, with much wailing and gnashing of teeth, suffered a one-trick set.

I caught up with Oliver at a prestigious London pairs tournament. I posed provocatively on his left, a buxom platinum blonde, modelled on a flame of his distant youth, Jean Harlow. But he didn't give me a second glance. I slipped away and returned as an equally gorgeous young man, but he remained unmoved. I recalled that the sexual powers of the human male peaked at the age of eighteen years, so Oliver's had been declining for at least seventy.

As I was surrounded by some of the world's finest, I took the opportunity to watch them in action, and perhaps identify another candidate for my omfoozle. I rejected Omar Sharif. (He had it coming.) His disappearance might be noticed. Bob Hamman worried me – too street-wise. Rodwell had possibilities, but how could I prise him away from Meckstroth?

Besides, all these players were all-rounders, generalists *par excellence*. I needed people with a single, perfectly developed talent, like a carrier pigeon. So I decided to stick with the venerable Oliver, but to change my tactics.

After the tournament, he was escorted to the front door of the hotel, where a taxi was usually waiting. But on this occasion, it was upstaged by a stately Rolls Royce.

"Compliments of the sponsor, Sir," said the uniformed chauffeur, and soon Oliver was gliding smoothly towards his London flat. After a few hundred metres, a cheerful cockney voice reached him through the intercom.

"I managed to pop in earlier, Sir." The chauffeur was evidently one of Britain's million bridge players. "I saw your joint top on board fourteen. Interesting use of spaghetti responses to the multi-two, Sir."

"Was that what we were playing?" he said. "I thought everything was natural."

I made a deferential noise, half way between a laugh and a cough. (Yes, you have guessed it – I was that chauffeur.) "Very good, Sir. But may I tell you my favourite of all your hands, Sir?"

I reminded him of one of his triumphs, sixty years previously. It should refute the theory that his brilliant departures from defensive orthodoxy sprang from his vast experience rather than his innate talent.

North/South Game. Dealer South.

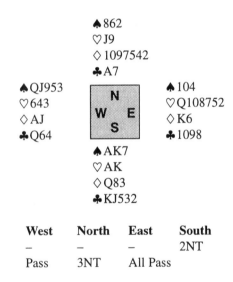

```
              ♠ 862
              ♡ J9
              ◇ 1097542
              ♣ A7
  ♠ QJ953         N        ♠ 104
  ♡ 643                    ♡ Q108752
  ◇ AJ        W     E      ◇ K6
  ♣ Q64          S         ♣ 1098
              ♠ AK7
              ♡ AK
              ◇ Q83
              ♣ KJ532
```

West	North	East	South
–	–	–	2NT
Pass	3NT	All Pass	

Oliver was East, with a hand offering slim potential for winning a brilliancy prize. The ♠Q was led and ducked. Declarer won the second round and led the ◇Q. West won with the ace and Oliver unblocked his king! Spades were cleared, and the ◇J provided West with an unexpected entry for his long spades.

Oliver received so many plaudits that he decided he could afford to be modest about it. "It stood out a mile," he told the editor of *Pre-War Bridge*.

"Obviously partner would have ducked the diamond with ace to three, and if he held ace-doubleton there was no chance. Our only hope was to establish the spade suit, and to do so I had to find partner with the diamond knave."

I asked Oliver whether he could remember his opponent's comments, but there was no reply. The old boy was fast asleep.

He never reached his flat, of course. I took him to my place, where I quickly took steps to ensure his immortality. (You will understand that the whereabouts of 'my place' must remain secret. I may wish to use it for future projects, and you are, as you have probably deduced, a prime candidate for omfoozling.)

While you are wondering what the fourth quality was, let me introduce you to Arthur, a dangerous underbidder and an uninspired technician, but, when it came to calculating the odds, a human computer.

It goes without saying that he could have bored for the Galaxy, but many bridge stars are not boring enough. Breathtaking coups may grab the headlines, but, in the words of Dr Paul Stern, matches are won by four dumb oxes (sic), playing straight down the middle.

I decided to bump into Arthur on the South Coast, where he was hosting a residential bridge weekend. Between duplicate sessions, he conducted seminars on fascinating mathematical aspects of the game. Most of his older clients attended; it was the only place in the hotel where they were sure to get a really good sleep.

Before slipping into the lecture, I admired myself in the vestibule mirror. I was a stereotypical librarian; thick spectacles obscuring the beauty of my deep blue eyes, and a shapeless hand-knitted frock hiding my exquisite curves. Nobody but Arthur, the supreme analyst, would notice my invisible assets.

He had written two hands on the whiteboard, and was offering his audience alternative lines of play.

"You will all agree," he intoned soporifically, "that there is a seventeen per-cent chance of both minor suits breaking." He paused to milk every ounce of drama from his next revelation. "The alternative line has nearly a nineteen per-cent probability of success, and is therefore clearly superior."

"Bravo!" I cried.

Half the room turned to stare at me. The other half woke up and automatically joined in the applause which I had led.

"Encore, master!" I demanded.

Dear Arthur! He stared at me, flushed with forty-nine per cent triumph and fifty-one per cent amazement. (He told me later that it was love at first sight, but perhaps that was just pillow talk.)

Like the twelve famous actors who played suspects in *Murder on the Orient Express*, I have deliberately misled you. You have concluded that I wanted Alfred for his arithmetical assets. Perish the thought. Even the most voluminous bridge books contain only a four or five page chapter about the odds, and little of it is of any use to a practical bridge player.

Here is an example of Arthur's ability to snatch defeat from the jaws of victory.

North/South Game. Dealer West.

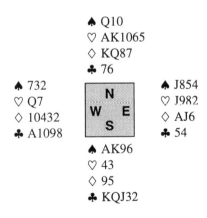

```
                    ♠ Q10
                    ♡ AK1065
                    ◇ KQ87
                    ♣ 76
    ♠ 732                          ♠ J854
    ♡ Q7          N                ♡ J982
    ◇ 10432    W     E             ◇ AJ6
    ♣ A1098       S                ♣ 54
                    ♠ AK96
                    ♡ 43
                    ◇ 95
                    ♣ KQJ32
```

West	North	East	South
Pass	1♡	Pass	2♣
Pass	2♦	Pass	3NT
All Pass			

In a Crockfords match, Arthur played in an excellent three no trump contract against strong opposition. At the other table, after an identical auction, a spade was led. This gave declarer six top tricks, and ample time to add three minor suit winners to his tally.

Against Arthur, West (clearly a disciple of Oliver) took note of his partner's failure to produce a spade overcall, and found the more daring lead of the ♡Q. Taking this card at face value, Arthur won on the table and advanced a club to his king. When this held, he crossed to the ♦K, which was also allowed to win the trick. A second round of clubs was captured by the ace, and West played the ♡7. Arthur was surprised, but not worried, when dummy's ten was headed by the jack.

At this point he was still confident, but when East shrewdly returned a spade, it became apparent that the cheap trick with the ♠10 was a Greek gift; the contract was no longer a virtual certainty. He recalculated the odds, and, for the want of anything better to do, cleared the hearts. The discards were rather troublesome, since he had potential winners in three suits. Reasonably enough, he pitched a club and a diamond, although this was to prove fatal. East persisted with spades, creating an insoluble entry problem.

Arthur did his best. He rose with the ♠A, and cashed the ♣J. When the clubs also failed to break, he calmly fired his last shot, the ♠K. If the knave appeared, he would still make the contract.

It didn't, and he didn't.

"Three no trumps was ninety-six-percent," he announced, in the tone of a man who had done what a man had to do. It was no disgrace to go down when you had played with Euclidean precision.

As a fine player yourself, you have probably spotted that Oliver or Ivor would have made short work of that contract. They would have envisaged the possibility that the opening lead might have been from shortage. And, at trick two, they would have played a low club from both hands. Now, even against best defence, declarer is home. (If you can see why within thirty seconds, do let me know. I might have a nice reward for you.)

So why did I want Arthur? Because, like Doctor Stern, I coveted the man's ox-like steadiness, his iron discipline. To paraphrase the Earl of Rochester's remark about Charles II, Arthur never chose a stupid line, and never saw a great one. The notion of his pulling a wrong card was preposterous. Revokes were not in his repertoire. Miscounting was for lesser mortals. He never forgot the system, the part score, or what had been played, by whom and when. Disasters left him unmoved. Distractions did not exist. Nothing deflected him from his purpose. He was Forest Gump.

Even his bridge betters (and there were many) envied Arthur's temperament, even though their more glamorous qualities and his metronomic reliability were mutually exclusive.

Except, of course, to the omfoozler.

The following morning, Arthur took me sailing in the English Channel. Neither boat nor bodies were ever seen again, which he would have found puzzling. The odds had been 37,000 to 1 on our returning safely.

♦ ♦ ♦ ♦ ♦

Valour is one of the primordial qualities of the master player, always provided that discretion is the better part of it. Fortunately, I already had Arthur, who possessed enough discretion for a regiment. I was now in a position to recruit the archetypal swashbuckler, and to Hell with the consequences!

I recalled the incomparable Errol Flynn, venturing coolly into Nottingham Castle, single-handedly decimating an entire Norman army, and escaping with head unbowed, hair unruffled, and green tights miraculously unladdered.

Now who in bridge was in that class?

It was while watching a Gold Cup match that I found the answer to that question. Lance didn't look like a man who would storm a castle single-handedly. He was a trifle too short for your regulation battlement-breacher. But I liked the rakish angle of the cigarette, poised lethally between his devil-may-care lips, and there was a hint of derring-do in the way he perched precariously on the extreme edge of his chair.

He sat South on the following deal. His opponents were notorious overbidders, but redoubtable card players, and Lance knew that to play safe against them meant slow but certain death.

North/South Game. Dealer West.

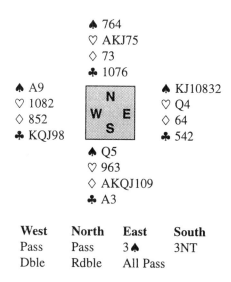

$\spadesuit$ 764
$\heartsuit$ AKJ75
$\diamondsuit$ 73
$\clubsuit$ 1076

$\spadesuit$ A9
$\heartsuit$ 1082
$\diamondsuit$ 852
$\clubsuit$ KQJ98

$\spadesuit$ KJ10832
$\heartsuit$ Q4
$\diamondsuit$ 64
$\clubsuit$ 542

$\spadesuit$ Q5
$\heartsuit$ 963
$\diamondsuit$ AKQJ109
$\clubsuit$ A3

West	North	East	South
Pass	Pass	3 $\spadesuit$	3NT
Dble	Rdble	All Pass	

East's three spades was forward, to say the least. Lance's vulnerable three no trumps was a fair speculation. If doubled, he could always remove to diamonds. North's redouble was a reasonable shot. It certainly put the spotlight on Lance.

Before the word 'cool' came to mean everything attractive to the younger generation, and vulgar to their elders (the youth of your planet is just like the youth of mine), it meant, amongst other things, the ability to take calculated risks without turning a hair. Lance's final pass was the ultimate exemplification of that quality.

As West considered his lead, I could sense his thoughts as though they were my own. The unsoundness of his partner's pre-empts were legendary. Both North and South were obviously prepared for a spade lead. It might even give them their ninth trick. And if, as seemed certain, they had the suit stopped, then East must hold some values in the other suits.

Pleased with his analysis, West led the ♣K. A couple of minutes later, Lance was recording a plus score of 2200. (His coolness did not extend to his risking the heart finesse.)

Sadly, Lance's team eventually lost by the narrowest of margins, but that redoubled game will be remembered long after the match result has been forgotten. I could have hugged him there and then, but I had to wait until after he had taken me for a Bangalore Phal curry. (Everything the man did was dicing with death.)

"Where have you been all my life?" he said, as his bright blue eyes smiled at me over the brandy glass.

"I was born the day I met you," I said. "I lived the few hours that I knew you. I died the moment you left me."

"My God!" He almost choked over his brandy. "Humphrey Bogart!"

This would have perplexed most women, and insulted others, but I knew just what he meant, "'In a Lonely Place,'" I said, naming a largely-forgotten, flawed masterpiece.

"Exactly. You must love the old ones."

"I once watched a thousand in less than a week," I said.

"That's impossible," he said.

"Not if you watch them twelve at a time," I said.

He laughed. Isn't it odd how the best way of disarming suspicion is to tell the absolute truth?

"What did you feel like when you passed your partner's redouble of three no trumps?" I asked.

"Totally relaxed," he said. "We'd been playing like wimps and losing steadily. We needed a big swing, and this was our chance."

This was the answer I wanted to hear. I could find a bevy of overbidding tearaways at any bridge club in the country, but Lance buckled his swash with great care. (Even Errol always made sure there was a back exit and a fast horse waiting.)

I was reminded of another deal from the match:

North/South Game. Dealer South.

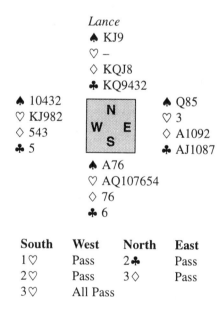

```
                        Lance
                        ♠ KJ9
                        ♡ –
                        ◇ KQJ8
                        ♣ KQ9432
        ♠ 10432                         ♠ Q85
        ♡ KJ982         N               ♡ 3
        ◇ 543        W     E            ◇ A1092
        ♣ 5             S               ♣ AJ1087
                        ♠ A76
                        ♡ AQ107654
                        ◇ 76
                        ♣ 6
```

South	West	North	East
1♡	Pass	2♣	Pass
2♡	Pass	3◇	Pass
3♡	All Pass		

"I loved your pass over three hearts," I said. "With a fifteen count opposite an opening bid it showed a lot of nerve."

"Nerve?" One well-groomed eyebrow arched expressively. "My partner seemed to think it was cowardly."

"Until the poor man went two off," I said. "But cowardice has more than one form, Lance. People are afraid of underbidding as well as overbidding."

"I never thought of that," he said. "I suppose you're right."

"I know I am. And nobody would have blamed you for going 3NT."

"With an aceless hand and a void in partner's suit?" He laughed. The sound was just right for a clearing in Sherwood Forest, but a decibel above the recommended level for a centre table in a cosy Indian restaurant.

"I agree with you entirely," I said. "Even Robin Hood believed in living to fight another day. What happened in the closed room?"

"You won't believe it." He winced at the memory. "The opposing North bid the regulation three no trumps, and my spineless team-mate in the East seat didn't even consider doubling."

I shook my head in sympathy. "I suppose South took out to four hearts?"

"He did. And guess what happened then?"

"Tell me."

"It was passed out."

"No!" I exclaimed, as loyally as Olivia de Havilland in *They Died With Their Boots On.*

"It was. Three off meant that we gained on the deal, but if we'd doubled we would have won the match."

"I wonder how you stand it?" I said.

"What?"

"The Merry Men."

"Ah!" His smile was tolerant. "They're all good players, until they're up against a team with a big reputation. Then they're shrinking bloody violets."

I considered pointing out the deficiency in his horticultural colour sense, but this was not the moment.

"How would you like to play with a top team?" I asked.

"I'd love it. All I need is a million and I'll hire the best five players alive."

"How odd," I said. "My idea is fairly similar, but rather less expensive."

His eyes met mine, which were a bewitching shade of hazel. "Do you know?" he said. "I actually believe you're serious."

"I am, but it's not a matter we should discuss in public."

"Where shall we go then?" His voice was hopeful. I couldn't bear to disappoint him.

"I know just the place," I said.

It was with some satisfaction that I took stock of what I had accumulated:

Ivor	Technique
Josephine	Will-to-win, controlled aggression
Oliver	Mental energy, stamina
Arthur	Temperament, reliability
Lance	Courage, coolness

I still needed one more talent. You might care to amuse yourself by trying to guess what it was.

Memory? Of course not. Winning at bridge is not like winning a pub quiz; any able player can acquire a memory compatible with world-class performance.

Table presence? A droll term which is to be found in any bridge work weighing more than a kilogram, and, as far as I'm concerned, it can jolly well stay there. It embraces so many disparate qualities that it has no significance for a serious omfoozler.

Card sense? Really! The suggestion is unworthy of you. Ely Culbertson used to maintain that card sense was a bugaboo invented by bad players to explain what would otherwise be regarded as their stupidity. (He later changed his mind, probably because he realised he had alienated half his readership.)

Instinct? Intuition? Psychology? That magical ability to locate missing queens in the absence of tangible indications? Much as I hate to destroy the illusions of a species obsessed with fortune tellers, clairvoyants and other pedlars of the paranormal, it is my duty to tell you that successful card placing can invariably be explained logically.

Consider this example of a truly fine card player in action.

Game All Dealer West.

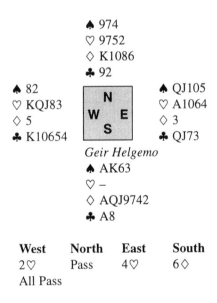

```
                    ♠ 974
                    ♡ 9752
                    ◇ K1086
                    ♣ 92
     ♠ 82                        ♠ QJ105
     ♡ KQJ83          N          ♡ A1064
     ◇ 5          W       E      ◇ 3
     ♣ K10654          S          ♣ QJ73
                 Geir Helgemo
                    ♠ AK63
                    ♡ –
                    ◇ AQJ9742
                    ♣ A8
```

West	North	East	South
2♡	Pass	4♡	6◇
All Pass			

West led the ♡K, ruffed by South. The only hope of making six diamonds appeared to depend on finding spades three-three, but the Norwegian declarer was alert for extra chances. He drew trumps in one round, and made the no-cost play of the ♠3 to the seven and jack. This catered for the possibility of what your deep thinkers call an intra finesse.

East was a deep thinker. After winning the trick with his deceptive jack, he concluded that declarer was fated to succeed. All he had to do was run the ♠9, pinning West's eight; then he could cross to dummy with a trump, and finesse the ♠6. So what could be done to divert declarer from finding this line? The answer came to East in a flash of inspiration. He put his opponent under immediate pressure by returning the ♠5.

At this point the odds favoured playing for a three-three spade break, but South viewed East's play with considerable interest. It was a most unnatural defence – surely a club was a standout. And East had won with the ♠J, which seemed suspiciously like a false-card. What was the fellow up to?

I was not present when declarer ran the spade lead round to dummy's nine, but I would have loved to have seen the expression on his face. It must have been like Pacino's in *The Scent of a Woman*, when he finished that tango without landing on his butt.

Would my creation play the hand with such commensurate ease? I am surprised you should ask such a question. Ivor would spot the potential intra finesse in a trice. Josephine's dominating presence would drive any East into making the same ill-considered spade return. Oliver would work out what his opponent was up to before his opponent did. Lance would coolly run the spade return to dummy's nine. And Arthur? Well, he would just keep serenely in the background, supporting his betters by making sure that nothing went wrong.

So forget individual talent and remember that bridge is a partnership game. Are we on the same wavelength? Good. Obviously, the final attribute was empathy.

Empathy has been described as the ability to see someone else's point of view, without necessarily agreeing with it. Sympathy is seeing and agreeing. When someone is being sick over the side of a ship, and you offer him an appropriate remedy, you have empathy. If you rush across to be sick with him, you have sympathy.

Over-sympathetic players will commiserate, not only with their partners' bad luck, but with their bad bridge. This is hardly a constructive pathway to improvement. (Not that you don't need the occasional touch of sympathy. There are times when it is diplomatic not to notice the mistakes of the fool opposite.)

Now you know why, for nearly two weeks, I had been scouring the tournament and rubber bridge scenes for somebody with the perfect balance. Most players were nice enough people, I suppose, until they found themselves with some cards in their hand and a partner in their gun-sights.

I was a nondescript, middle-aged man, sitting in the back of a taxi, which was crawling through a traffic jam towards a well-known London club. A motor cyclist, who was delivering pizzas, cut in front of the driver, forcing him to brake suddenly. I waited for the inevitable shower of invective.

"Poor fellow," said the taxi driver.

"I beg your pardon?" I said.

"If the pizza doesn't get to the customer on time, a pound is deducted from the bill. It comes out of the poor bugger's wages."

"Really?" I struggled to conceal my stupefaction.

Just then a tourist strolled alongside the cab and thrust his head rudely through the driver's window.

"Where's Green Street?" he asked abruptly.

"First right, second left, mate."

The tourist gave a perfunctory nod, and departed without comment.

"Not exactly a model of politeness," I sympathised.

"I suppose not," the driver gave a tolerant smile.

"Don't you get a bit fed up with being asked the way to places?" I empathised.

"Sometimes," he admitted. "But then I reckon that every time a taxi driver is kind to a pedestrian, that pedestrian becomes a bit more likely to use a taxi."

By the Great Galactic Spirit, I was undoubtedly in the presence of a saint! I had only one more question to ask my new friend.

"Do you, by any chance, play bridge?"

He turned round to get a good look at me. "My friend," he said. "Not only do I play bridge, but you are in the presence of the current holder of the West Tooting Mixed Pairs Championship."

"You don't say!" I said, rejoicing inwardly. It wasn't exactly the Bermuda Bowl final, but it definitely qualified. And if he didn't know how to take a finesse, no matter. Ivor would take the finesses.

As I prepared for the final stage of my experiment, I experienced an uncanny sense of foreboding. I reminded myself that I was a scientist, a natural philosopher. But so was Frankenstein. And look what happened to him.

I shuddered. I had been on Earth for far too long. Superstition had me in its thrall. I confronted it with remorseless logic. I reminded myself of Mary Shelley's title of her Gothic extravagance, *Frankenstein, or the Modern Prometheus*. And Prometheus was the embodiment of all the human virtues.

I laughed virtuously. This was much better, I was worthy of the name. I was about to create a matchless bridge player, not a vengeful monster who would pursue me relentlessly across the world's oceans, like Gregory Peck in *Moby Dick*.

The Gothic mood evaporated. I flicked the switch that opened the chamber from which my creation would appear. As the door swung open, I felt an unfamiliar thrill of anticipation.

And then it happened. *He* emerged. I stared in horror, as a pair of mesmeric eyes rapidly scanned their surroundings, then settled on me. Their penetrating gaze told me that he knew who I was and what I had done, and was not impressed. I shuddered helplessly as he advanced towards me. Somehow I knew that any illusion I projected would crumble before that overwhelming intellect. For the first time, I began to realise the enormity of what I had done. Prometheus had been punished for stealing the fire of the gods. Was I face-to-face with the instrument of their revenge?

He took another menacing step. I cringed, as his mouth opened to pronounce my doom.

"Hello," he said. "My name is Tony Forrester."

3
YOUR DEAL, MR BOND

1
An Interview with M

James Bond's right hand, hard and straight as a plank, whipped towards the Italian's windpipe. It landed with a satisfying thud. He pulled out his Beretta and tapped it with clinical precision against the unprotected skull. As the black-clad figure slumped to the floor, Bond became aware of the ring of faces staring at him with shocked expressions. Had the savage nature of his response been a trifle over the top? Perhaps, but one thing was for sure – he would never be overcharged in that restaurant again.

Twenty minutes later, his vermillion supercharged 1923 Bentley roared to an unobtrusive halt at the tall, gaunt building he loved and loathed. He took the elevator to the top floor, and thought nostalgically of the days when he had mounted the sixteen flights of stairs four at a time – five if someone was watching.

"He's waiting, James." The faithful Miss Moneypenny wagged an admonishing finger at the wall clock, which told him he was two minutes late. He gave her a fighting grin, and strolled through the double doors, trying not to look like an errant fourth former reporting for six of the best.

M's cold blue eyes looked at him, through him. "Better sit down, 007. You look awful."

Bond couldn't disagree. He squinted at his chief through a bloodshot haze, while the grandmother of all headaches vanquished a double dose of Phensic with contemptuous ease.

M's expression was bleakly calculating, as if he were sizing up a racehorse and slowly realising it was a donkey. "How's your bridge?" he asked abruptly.

Bond ran a furry tongue along the service dentist's latest orthodontic masterpiece. "Not bad, Sir. Aches a little after a few iced vodkas, but otherwise...."

M gave a vexed snort. "Not your teeth, man, the card game. How's your form?"

Bond sweated as he recalled his last performance at Blades; the lunatic sacrifices, the drunken revokes, the kindergarten miscounting and, worst of all, the supercilious sympathy of his partners. Should he tell M the awful truth? For a moment he wavered. Then he remembered he was an officer of the British Navy, sailing in the glorious wake of Drake, Nelson and Jellicoe.

"Absolutely godlike, Sir."

"Oh? Then the report that you dropped fifteen hundred pounds the other night was blasphemous."

Bond was used to the Section prying into his sex life, his bank overdraft and, for all he knew, his toilet habits, but it wasn't cricket when a man couldn't enjoy a spot of privacy in his bridge club. "I held tram tickets all evening," he said lamely.

"You had five slams, Bond. And floored every one of them." M paused to light his pipe. He didn't invite Bond to smoke, a sure sign of grade A disapproval.

"If you say so, Sir."

"Try not to floor this one." M slid a sheet of paper across the desk. It contained two bridge hands.

♠ J93
♡ 854
◇ K82
♣ A752

♠ AKQ107
♡ 97
◇ AQ54
♣ 96

"You are South," M continued. "Four spades is the contract. A half-way decent one for a change. The heart king is led, followed by the queen. East overtakes and continues with the knave."

Bond's eyes narrowed as he took in the deal. It was a bitch of a problem, particularly after those two bottles of lunch-time Chianti and the wild night with that nubile nurse and her randy aunt. To hell with it, he decided, and lit a defiant cigarette.

M's eyes grew colder, bluer, but he didn't press charges. He could afford to swallow a dose of grade D insolence from an agent who had become a mere shadow of his former self. Bond filled his lungs from his thirty-first Balkan Sobranie of the day, and wondered if he'd ever been a former self.

"Well, 007?"

"Nothing much to this one, Sir. I ruff, draw trumps and reel off the diamonds. If they're three-three, I'm home and dry. If not, I pray for a revoke."

"This deal illustrates a fairy common theme." M was crisp, lucid, insufferable. "It has been used by Charles Goren and others to show the difference between a poor player, an average player and a master. Welcome to the first category."

"Thank you, Sir." Bond blew a smoke ring of pure insurrection. Then his hidden rage worked like a tonic; suddenly he saw the master play. "I'd draw two rounds of trumps," he said. "Then I'd tackle diamonds. Even if they're four-two, the opponent with the doubleton might be out of trumps."

"Congratulations, 007. You've advanced to average. But I'm afraid he isn't out of trumps."

"Really, Sir?" Bond shrugged. "Then the contract is unmakeable."

M puffed complacently. "Saladin made it."

Bond blocked the fast service. "Good for him, Sir." He didn't know Saladin from salad cream, but he was too wily a trout to rise to such an obvious bait.

M, every inch the Compleat Angler, handed Bond a copy of the complete deal and proceeded inplacably.

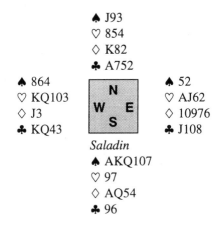

"Saladin ruffed, and ducked a club, the key play. The defence was now helpless. In practice, a diamond was returned. Saladin took in hand." M regarded Bond like a judge giving an old lag every chance. "You can see what happened next of course."

Bond expelled a lethal mixture of Chianti fumes, CO_2 and nicotine. "Vaguely, Sir."

"Saladin crossed to the club ace and ruffed a club with the queen. He cashed the ace of trumps, crossed to dummy's diamond king and ruffed the last club high. Now he overtook his carefully preserved spade ten with the knave, and drew the last trump with dummy's nine. The diamond queen provided the tenth trick." M eyed Bond benevolently as he delivered the *coup de grâce.* "And he did it all in ninety seconds flat."

Bond was livid. It was a straightforward dummy reversal. In his salad days he'd have spotted it standing on his head. Which was a good way to spot dummy reversals, he reflected wryly.

"You used to be the best declarer in the Department." M's voice was gruff as he blew his nose into a matching red handkerchief. "Now let me tell you about Saladin."

Bond struggled to keep his end up. "Any relation to the fellow who got his nose bloodied by Richard the Lionheart?"

"Not impossible." M seemed pleasantly surprised by Bond's smidgeon of 'O' Level history. "Chap's a mystery. Rose without trace ten years ago. Grey eminence behind all the shady financial headlines – currency manipulation, hocus pocus with futures." He jerked his pipe sideways, his favourite gesture of distaste. "That's just his respectable side. If a money man can ever be respectable."

"If indeed, Sir." Bond mustered a thin smile. He was never sure when M was making a joke, but it was best to be on the safe side.

"Parasites, 007." M looked out of the window with that glassy stare which warned Bond there was an aphorism coming. "Who said that a man's darkest hour is when he decides to get money without earning it?"

Here was a chance for some grade A toadying. "Sound a bit like you, Sir."

"No." M shook his head. "What I said was that God shows his contempt for money by the kind of people he selects to receive it."

Bond's hair rose. M mentioned God only in times of dire national emergency. Normally he was strict Church of England.

"According to our man in Istanbul, the vulture is spreading his wings. Sex, drugs, extortion. The word is he's just about replaced SPECTRE."

Bond's pulse raced at the mention of his old enemy. Was he booked for another thrilling life or death struggle? Or was there still time to wangle a month's sick leave? Fibrositis of the trigger finger was usually a good bet.

"Does this mean...?"

"Yes, 007, I'm afraid it does. Usual code one crisis. Nuclear devices smuggled into all the European capitals. To be detonated by long-range radio signals in six weeks time."

Bond wondered where to spend his sick leave. Hawaii seemed a sound choice. He said, "There must be an unless, Sir."

"Unless each of the powers concerned comes up with twenty billion dollars."

Bond attempted an incredulous whistle, but his upper lip was too stiff. "To Saladin?" he asked.

"According to our man in Athens. No proof of course."

"But what has all this to do with bridge, Sir?"

"I'm coming to that." M puffed out irritable clouds of pipe smoke. "Saladin owns an island in the Eastern Mediterranean."

"Owns it, Sir?"

"Bought it, lock, stock and barrel. Renamed it Saladinos, and turned it into a bloody fortress."

Things must be desperate, thought Bond. M hadn't used the B word since the Gulf War. "Does he ever leave it, Sir?"

"No. And the only visitors allowed are bridge players, one at a time. He pays them a fortune, so they have to be world-beaters. Pity you don't qualify."

That one was well below the belt. Bond was only too aware that it was five years since he'd last saved the world. He'd been deleted from the KGB Christmas card list. Junior colleagues who used to hold him in awe had started to leave their cars in his parking space. His photograph was still on the office wall, but the secretaries had erased the "best agent we ever had" caption.

M watched him stonily, "How long have you been with the Service, James?"

Whenever M used his first name, Bond mentally pressed the red alert button. "I've a rotten memory for dates," he hedged.

"Then we won't mention them." M was cheerful, avuncular, dangerous. "I've managed to scotch a rumour that your original appointment was approved by Gladstone."

This was one joke Bond refused to laugh at. Or was it a joke? M's pipe had gone out. He relit it with consummate lethargy, a big cat spinning out his game with the passé mouse. Bond waited tensely, struggling to recall the small print in his pension plan.

"Of course a lot can happen in five or six weeks, James. You might even become a world-class bridge player."

The doors opened, as if by pre-arrangement, and Q entered.

"Ah, there you are, 007. Now please pay attention." The Department's gadget master regarded social niceties with the same lack of affection as a fastidious lamp-post might have regarded dogs. He handed Bond a pair of designer spectacles.

"I don't need glasses." Bond was inordinately proud of his other unimpaired faculty.

"They're not a normal pair, 007. Put them on."

Bond complied, with a smile of good-humoured contempt perfected over several decades of belittling Q's inventions. M gave him thirteen playing cards, and placed a similar number in front of him, face up.

"That, 007, is your dummy. Overbidding as usual, you have reached a small slam in spades. The club king is led. Saladin is your partner, and the fate of Europe may depend on your impressing him." M gave a hand to Q, and kept one for himself, as Bond grimly assessed his chances.

Love All. Dealer East.

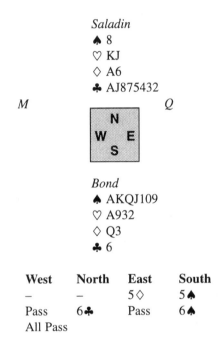

Saladin
♠ 8
♡ KJ
◇ A6
♣ AJ875432

Bond
♠ AKQJ109
♡ A932
◇ Q3
♣ 6

West	North	East	South
–	–	5◇	5♠
Pass	6♣	Pass	6♠
All Pass			

Bond placed the ♣A on the king, and glared sourly at Q when he discarded a diamond. So trumps are six-nil, he thought, or Q would have ruffed.

"And I can't have any diamonds, or I'd surely have led one," said M, reading his thoughts.

"Really, Sir?" Bond seethed. "I'm afraid that's a bit advanced for me."

"Then I'll confirm the obvious. My shape is six-three-nil-four." M was having a field day. "So you can't make the contract unless my hearts are precisely queen, ten, small."

"Yes, Sir. The penny had actually dropped."

"And even then, having drawn trumps before taking the heart finesse, there seems to be no way of getting back to hand to enjoy the long heart. Any ideas, 007?"

"None that I'd care to make public." Bond wouldn't have ventured a turnip on his chances. He gritted his teeth. "Sir," he added poisonously.

"Clearly you need some more help." M pressed a button on his intercom. Suddenly Bond felt an intermittent tingling near his left ear. He was about to pull off the spectacles, when a gesture from Q stopped him.

"I'm ashamed of you, 007. Can't you recognise Morse? Leave them where they are and try to decipher it."

Q was right. A morse signal was barely descernible in the left arm of his spectacles. A two-letter message, E and S. But what did it mean?

M's weatherbeaten face was creased with enjoyment. "In view of the need to draw trumps, I should have thought that the eight of spades might spring to mind."

Swearing profoundly, Bond played that card from the table, and Q discarded another diamond. The next signal was N-S. That was easy – the nine of spades. His selection was rewarded with an ironic 'Well done' from M.

The predictable A-S signal followed. He obediently advanced the ace of spades and was wondering what to throw from dummy when the message A-D instructed him to jettison the diamond ace! Following orders like a zombie, he drew the rest of the trumps, finessed ♡J and cashed ♡K. But the ensuing I-D signal completely foxed him, until M handed him a printed card:

Ace	A	Seven	S
King	K	Six	I
Queen	Q	Five	F
Jack	J	Four	O
Ten	T	Three	H
Nine	N	Two	W
Eight	E		

"Very clever, Sir." It was Bond's turn with the heavy sarcasm. "To avoid duplication, you've used the second letter of four of the lower denominations." Not bad for a has been, he thought smugly, and led the six of diamonds from the table. Q rose with the king, but, holding only red cards, he was forced to give declarer the lead and the last three tricks.

The full deal was:

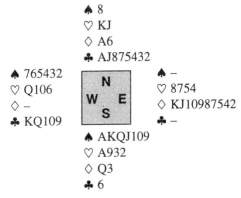

```
                     ♠ 8
                     ♡ KJ
                     ◇ A6
                     ♣ AJ875432
     ♠ 765432                      ♠ -
     ♡ Q106           N            ♡ 8754
     ◇ -          W       E        ◇ KJ10987542
     ♣ KQ109          S            ♣ -
                     ♠ AKQJ109
                     ♡ A932
                     ◇ Q3
                     ♣ 6
```

"Brilliant dummy play," said M, with satisfaction.

"Thank you, Sir." Bond was genuinely touched.

"Not you, 007. Plum!"

"Plum, Sir?" Bond kept a straight face as he picked up the gauntlet. "Not one of the Victoria Plums?"

"Plum Meredith," M replied heavily. "A world champion and one of the finest declarers ever to draw trumps. I watched him play that hand. It was forty years ago, but it seems like yesterday."

A nauseatingly nostalgic silence followed. Bond put it to good use by examining his fingernails and ignoring Q. He was rewarded by the note of wounded pride in the forthcoming lecture.

"The camera in those spectacles, 007, is a miracle of miniaturisation. Everything you view through them is transmitted instantly to our operator along the corridor. He sends back morse messages to the state-of-the-art receiver near your left ear. And nobody else will hear – they're for your ears only."

"Interesting." Bond inspected the glasses with a bored air. "I believe I saw a similar pair in British Home Stores."

"We can do without the frozen adolescence, 007."

This scurrilous term had been used by the service psychologist to describe Bond's chronic childishness. But he had avenged the slander by filling the shrink's overcoat pockets with a quart of canteen custard.

Now he turned his fury on M, for remembering the slur. "One thing you seem to have overlooked, Sir. I accept that our backroom boys will be able to see the cards. But how will they know the bidding, or the final contract?"

M waved his pipe, as though brushing off an educationally subnormal fly. "We'll have a radio transmitter hidden in your pocket handkerchief." He walked over to his European war map, a relic from 1943. Swastikas still covered most of Europe. Was Moneypenny falling down on the job? Or was it a symptom of M's neo-Fascism? He fingered a miniscule dot, somewhere East of Rhodes.

"This is Saladinos. You will arrive there by invitation in five weeks time. You will play bridge with your host, guided by a famous expert from an off-shore submarine. You will then exploit your privileged position to discover the transmitter that controls the nuclear bombs, neutralise it, and destroy Saladinos and everything on it. Any questions?"

"Just one, Sir. Is my escape by any chance included in the plan?"

M's pipe described a casual circle. "That's optional."

"Nice to have the choice, Sir. One other point. How are you going to get Saladin to invite me?"

"Oh, didn't I mention it? You are going as Zia Mahmood. He has a standing invitation, which so far he hasn't taken up."

Bond froze in the act of lighting Sobranie number thirty-three. "But I look nothing like him. I don't sound like him. I don't move like him. I don't think like him."

Q stepped into the breach. "You will, 007. We'll get at least a stone off your weight. The rest is a simple matter of wigs, sun tan lamps, a spot of latex and a good drama coach. I'm sure you've seen *Mission Impossible*."

"We'll take twenty years off you, James." M seemed almost excited. Was sending men to almost certain death a sex surrogate? "The biggest problem was how to get you to play like Zia. Saladin's never met him, but he'll know his style."

"But we've solved that one," said Q.

M said, "We have. Zia's going to be our man in the submarine."

"I see, Sir."

"And one more thing. Saladin is what the Americans call a culture vulture. Reads Marcel Proust for fun, spouts epigrams by the dozen, all that."

"Not exactly my forté, Sir."

"No." M agreed with infuriating alacrity. "Fortunately we've got five weeks to civilise you."

"I shall look forward to that, Sir," said Bond frigidly.

2
Journey to Saladinos

James Bond was met at Rhodes Airport by a stunning blonde. She was tall, at least five feet ten inches, most of it legs. A white mini-skirt covered almost an inch of them. Her face inspired lascivious memories of the Sixties, his peak period. She reminded him of Grace Kelly, but the alluring curl of her shocking pink lips hinted that she was far more accessible.

"Mr Mahmood, welcome to Rhodes."

His trained ear detected a slight Estonian accent, with a trace of Southern Bulgarian.

"My name is Colette."

And probably French, he added shrewdly.

"I am Saladin's private secretary," she continued. "And your biggest fan."

This was a promising start. As he was ushered into a sleek limousine, Bond decided that the gruelling weeks of wheat germ, carrot juice and voice coaching had been worth it. But he would kill for a cigarette. Colette listened in rapt admiration to his well-rehearsed bridge anecdotes, until the car glided to a halt and they transferred to the helicopter which would take them to Saladinos.

"Have you flown in a helicopter before?" she asked.

"Several times."

"Good. Then perhaps I can amuse you with a hand I played last week."

She lowered her eyes demurely, the humble acolyte before the guru. "Actually I've been saving it for you."

He gazed down without enthusiasm at the Mediterranean at its bluest, as she produced the inevitable, doom-laden piece of paper. Any problem she'd saved for Zia would be way beyond the fading star of the Secret

Service. Would those sleepless nights cramming *Ask Zia* and *Bridge My Way* prove enough?

East/West Game. Dealer South.

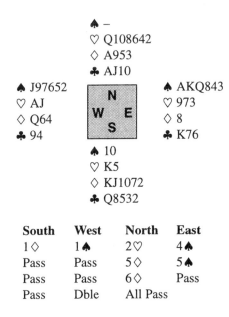

	♠ —	
	♡ Q108642	
	◇ A953	
	♣ AJ10	

♠ J97652		♠ AKQ843
♡ AJ		♡ 973
◇ Q64		◇ 8
♣ 94		♣ K76

	♠ 10	
	♡ K5	
	◇ KJ1072	
	♣ Q8532	

South	West	North	East
1◇	1♠	2♡	4♠
Pass	Pass	5◇	5♠
Pass	Pass	6◇	Pass
Pass	Dble	All Pass	

"I ruffed the spade lead," Colette told him. "The opponents had bid up to the five level on slender values."

"So they must have some shape," Bond interjected, at the top of his form.

"Exactly. So I played a diamond to the king and continued with the jack, intending to run it." She looked at Bond as though seeking his approval. He responded with an inscrutable nod. "But he *covered*," she added.

"I see." His smile was suitably sphinx-like.

"So I won in dummy, and led a heart to the king and ace." She paused. Bond sensed there was a key play coming. He leaned forward, every sense alert. "West immediately switched to the four of clubs," Colette told him.

"Decision time," he observed. It seemed a safe enough thing to say.

"I know, and I got it wrong. I took the club finesse. One off," she said ruefully. "Now you must tell me how I should have played."

Bond knew he had more chance of telling her the names of the forty-nine deputy high priests of the fourth Aztec dynasty. Had she seen through his disguise and resolved to test him? He fished through his memory and came up with a hoary old marron glacé from his basic training manual – the Boomerang!

"My dear Colette, you've had several days to think about it. I'm sure you can tell *me* how to play it." He was Socrates, towering over the young Plato. "Can't you now?"

"I hope so." She was dying to show off to her hero – it wasn't a trap. "The clue I missed was West's gratuitous cover of the diamond jack."

"Ah!" he said, oozing artificial intelligence from every pore.

Colette said, "It was a clever defence. Had he not covered, I would have run the jack. When it held, I would have led a low heart towards the table, and the fall of the jack would have shown me that I didn't need the club finesse."

"So?" Interrogative monosyllables were an essential component of the Boomerang.

"So I should have given West the credit for a far-sighted play, read him for the ace-jack of hearts, and risen with the club ace."

"Good girl." What a relief! If he had been forced to blow his cover, he'd have been compelled to kill her, overpower the pilot, fly back to Rhodes and abort the mission.

And that, he concluded, as an air pocket threw them together and her heady perfume played Monopoly with his libido, would have been a tragic waste.

3
The Island

Saladinos was a steep green hill, rising menacingly from the ocean. It reminded Bond of a Triton, warning ships to brave the hazardous reefs at their peril. He may have spent his boyhood classics lessons surreptitiously reading comics, but he'd seen *Jason and the Argonauts* nine times. A well-kept road climbed, like a spiral staircase, to the spectacular white villa near the summit.

The helicopter landed, and a very tall man stood watching them as they descended the steps brought by two muscular Greeks, who looked like all-in wrestlers and probably were.

"Zia!" The tall man's voice was deep and commanding. "I know I can call you Zia. And you must call me Saladin. Colette must have told you how much I admire you."

"I'm sure it will be mutual." Bond looked up at his host, six feet six inches of Spartan leanness, draped in a dazzling white silk suit. Yet Saladin was satanically dark, with eyes as black as the pits of hell. Bond compared the cruel, handsome face with the faces of his other enemies. When Blofield and company had threatened to blow up a continent or two, it was just business. For Saladin it would be an amusing pastime.

A third wrestler carried Bond's luggage, while he followed with Saladin and admired the priceless paintings which flanked the magnificent Renaissance staircase. Bond paused at a perfect replica of the Mona Lisa. As usual she was smiling at him like the queen of spades.

"A fine copy," he said.

Saladin appraised him coolly. "Why should you think it is a copy?"

That one had a lot of curve on it, so Bond let it go by. He was ushered into a room that was a sybarite's paradise. If he sold his Bentley, his London flat, and even the uncensored version of his memoirs, the proceeds wouldn't pay for a wall of it.

He searched for hidden mirrors and bugs, found none, showered, shaved, tarted up his elaborate make-up, did a couple of press-ups and felt ready to take on the world. He checked his spectacles and radio transmitter, strolled down the staircase, winked knowingly at the Mona Lisa, and was met by a butler, who took him to a spacious salon where Saladin and Colette were waiting.

Saladin rose majestically, and why not? On his own island the man was king. Better to rule in Saladinos than serve in Heaven, Bond mused, and the Mephistophelian conceit seemed chillingly apt.

"I hope you are in a champagne mood, Zia." Saladin opened a bottle with strong deft fingers, and said, "I acquired this vineyard ten years ago. After a few improvements, I believe it now produces the wine which Dom Perignon merely aspires to be."

"I've always preferred Tattinger." As soon as he uttered the words, Bond could have kicked himself. Tattinger was his trade mark, not Zia's. He watched Saladin pour three glasses, and smiled at Colette, who seemed to smile back with her whole body.

"To bridge!" Saladin toasted.

Bond added gallantly, "And women!"

"And champagne," said Saladin. "I see you know your Belloc."

Bond struggled to remember what a belloc was, while his host began to recite.

> "The accursed power which stands on privilege,
> And goes with women and champagne and bridge,
> Broke, and democracy resumed her reign,
> Which goes with bridge and women and champagne."

"Exactly." Bond still hadn't identified a belloc, so he nodded sagely, sipped reverently and panned his memory for a fitting compliment. He came up with gold! "This wine should be drunk kneeling, with head bared."

Saladin asked, "Didn't Dumas say that about Montrachet?"

Bond replied, "Frequently," and was rewarded by a grin from Saladin and a chuckle from Colette.

"By the way, Zia, I have been fascinated by a hand you played recently." Saladin recited the deal with dazzling rapidity. It was far too rapid for Bond, who prayed that it was one of the hands he had memorised.

Zia
♠ J52
♡ J10943
◇ –
♣ KJ853

♠ K10943   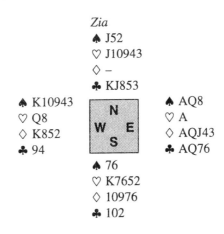   ♠ AQ8
♡ Q8   ♡ A
◇ K852   ◇ AQJ43
♣ 94   ♣ AQ76

♠ 76
♡ K7652
◇ 10976
♣ 102

West	North	East	South
Pass	Pass	2♣	Pass
2♠	Pass	3◇	Pass
4◇	Pass	4NT(i)	Pass
5◇(ii)	Pass	5NT	Pass
6◇(iii)	Pass	7♠	All Pass

(i)   RKCB
(ii) One of the five aces
(iii) One extra king

"As the cards lay, Zia, the grand slam is frigid, yet you defeated it. I know how you played, but I would be fascinated to know your reasoning. Apparently you led a heart, and dummy's ace won the first trick."

Bond felt his pulse rate leap into three figures. By sheer luck, he recalled the hand from his nocturnal cramming, but could he explain it with convincing fluency? Zia would be on duty, but Morse was far too slow for the purpose. It was up to 007.

"As an exercise," he drawled, "the deal might have made chapter two of the Idiot's Guide to Card Reading. For his spade bid, declarer must have five to the king. For his diamond raise, he probably has king to three or four. So a heart ruff or a winning club finesse gives him his thirteenth trick." Bond was painfully aware that he was beginning to run out of ammunition, but Saladin charged to the rescue.

"A succinct analysis, Zia. Now check my interpretation of the unfortunate declarer's thought process. Ruffing a heart is fraught with traffic problems and other dangers. So he decides to improve his chances by playing the ace of spades and crossing to the king."

Saladin paused for approval. Bond wondered why so many bridge players liked to show off to the genuine stars. For the same reason people were stupid enough to tell jokes to professional comedians, he supposed. So he gave the arrogant swine a thin smile of encouragement.

"If the jack drops," Saladin proceeded, "he will confidently ruff a heart, return to hand via the diamond king, draw the last trump and claim. But if the jack doesn't appear, he will fall back on the club finesse. Am I right?"

With a single bound, Bond was out of the quicksand. "Absolutely," he said. "And you know what Confucius said – when declarer is about to bring home bacon, tempt him with slice of poisoned turkey."

"So, Zia, on the second round of trumps, you dropped a poisonous jack."

"Yes. Declarer's sigh of relief would have done justice to a fat lady peeling off an over-tight corset. He ruffed a heart with dummy's queen, and led a small diamond from the table. I ruffed. The fat lady sang. It was all over."

"T.I.C.K," Zia was signalling his approval through the magic spectacles.

"Wonderful," Colette's eyes were shining.

Saladin said, "I agree. Byron was wrong when he said drinking was a pause from thinking." He coiled a long arm around Bond's shoulders. "Colette, more champagne."

Bond knew he should quit while he was ahead, but he was on a roll. He finished his glass and nodded his thanks when Colette replenished it. "When asked what my favourite wine is, I usually say 'someone else's'."

Colette joined in. "W.C. Fields claimed that his two favourite wines were red and white."

"And my two favourite suits are red and black." Bond made a crude attempt to change the subject before he gave himself away by asking for a Martini, shaken but not stirred.

"Which must be our cue to play some bridge." Saladin glanced at Colette, who excused herself. "We have time for a rubber or two before we dine."

Bond watched Colette leave the room, moving like a super-model on her own private cat-walk. "A lovely lady," he said.

"Very." Saladin spoke without warmth, as though Colette, like one of his paintings, was just another possession.

Bond said, "I congratulate you."

"Thank you, Zia. She would make a fine *courtisane de marque*, would she not? My relationship with Colette is not a physical one, however."

Bond instantly recalled a bizarre circumstance. When Colette had alighted from the helicopter, the tall man had not even glanced at her legs. He suddenly became aware that the long arm was still round his shoulders, and began to wonder if he had used too much Paco Rabanne.

"My dear Zia," Saladin laughed mirthlessly, "I religiously avoid all forms of sex, from onanism to pluralism. They would divert me from my two great passions, bridge and the pursuit of power."

Bond said, "Mine are bridge and the pursuit of happiness."

"Not power?"

"Not especially, Saladin."

"What is bridge but the perfect vehicle for exercising power? Power, as you know, is the capacity to influence the behaviour of others. You drop one of your celebrated deceptive nines, and your opponent misplays fatally. You preempt in hearts, he reaches a grand slam in spades, and naturally places your partner with the queen, but of course you hold it, otherwise you would not have preempted. I know all about you, you see. Your victim has as much chance of exercising free will as a rabbit transfixed by the hypnotic gaze of a stoat."

"You forget one thing, Saladin. Just as the stoat eats the rabbit, my deceptions usually win money."

"That is incidental. You could probably recall all your favourite coups at the drop of a hat. But the results of the rubbers concerned? I doubt it."

"How right you are." Bond sensed it was time to lose gracefully.

Colette returned in the company of a short, squat, studious-looking man, with horn-rimmed spectacles and a head of magnificently unblemished baldness.

"Allow me to present Stavros." Saladin gave the man's shiny pate a proprietorial pat. "My valued colleague, a financial wizard and our fourth for bridge. His play is remarkably consistent, Zia. It is utterly free from blemish or brilliancy."

Bond grasped a limp, moist hand. "I envy you, Stavros. I've managed to weed out blemish but brilliancy is proving remarkably stubborn."

4
The Early Skirmishing

Battle lines were drawn up. They agreed a modest list of conventions –
Stayman, Blackwood, the Unusual No Trump. They cut for partners. Bond
drew Colette.

Each side had gone down in slightly ambitious games when the following
deal provided an opportunity for a stubborn brilliancy.

Dealer South. Love All.

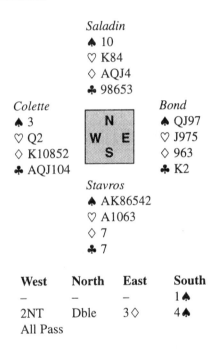

Saladin
- ♠ 10
- ♡ K84
- ◇ AQJ4
- ♣ 98653

Colette
- ♠ 3
- ♡ Q2
- ◇ K10852
- ♣ AQJ104

Bond
- ♠ QJ97
- ♡ J975
- ◇ 963
- ♣ K2

Stavros
- ♠ AK86542
- ♡ A1063
- ◇ 7
- ♣ 7

West	North	East	South
–	–	–	1♠
2NT	Dble	3◇	4♠
All Pass			

Bond regarded artificial bids with a degree of contempt he usually
reserved for powdered mashed potatoes. He shuddered when Zia's signal
forced him to bid three diamonds. This might have cost him five hundred.
Instead he found himself defending a far from simple four spade contract.

The defence began with two rounds of clubs. Stavros ruffed and played
three rounds of trumps. On lead, Bond was considering cashing his fourth

spade when the letters N-D suggested a seemingly fatuous alternative. Had Zia gone mad? Probably, but Bond's orders were to obey the signals without question, so he flicked the ◇9 petulantly onto the table.

Stavros raised his eyebrows at the remarkable switch. In dummy with the ◇J, He cashed the ◇A, ruffed a club and then threw Bond in with a trump. Bond wanted to exit with a low heart, but another moronic instruction from Zia told him to advance the ♡9. By an amazing stroke of luck, this did no damage to the defence; the nine was covered by the ten and queen, but declarer still had to lose a heart for a one trick defeat.

"Magnificent, Zia." Whatever else Saladin was, he was a good loser. "Your lead of the diamond nine broke up the minor suit squeeze. Most experts would have found that play but your subsequent choice of the nine of hearts was masterly."

"Or lucky," Stavros muttered sourly.

"Stavros, I am ashamed of you. I know you have Beethoven's eye for painting and Van Gogh's ear for music. Now I learn that you also possess Mrs Guggenheim's flair for bridge. The nine of hearts breaks up a classic guard squeeze. If Zia had cashed his master trump before switching to a diamond you could have reached this end position."

"Y.A.W.N." Zia signalled. "N.E.X.T. D.E.A.L." he added for good measure, as Saladin swiftly wrote the four-card ending onto the back of his score card:

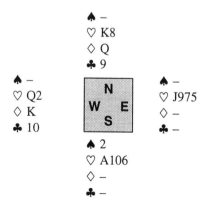

"The lead of your last trump would squeeze Colette in three suits. Come on, Stavros. Acknowledge the fact. Show us that your IQ is higher than your blood temperature."

Stavros agreed sulkily.

Bond said, "Saladin, I must thank you for your generous analysis. I had no idea I was that good." He paused humbly. "But you finally convinced me."

Then, after each side had scored an easy game, Stavros dealt a hand which was to provide him with a chance of self-redemption.

Dealer South. Game All.

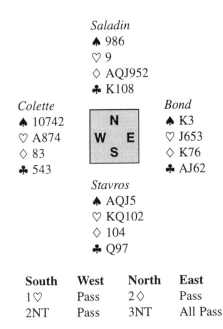

Saladin
♠ 986
♡ 9
◇ AQJ952
♣ K108

Colette
♠ 10742
♡ A874
◇ 83
♣ 543

Bond
♠ K3
♡ J653
◇ K76
♣ AJ62

Stavros
♠ AQJ5
♡ KQ102
◇ 104
♣ Q97

South	West	North	East
1♡	Pass	2◇	Pass
2NT	Pass	3NT	All Pass

Colette led the ♠2 to the king and ace. Stavros ran the ◇10 and continued the suit, losing to the king. As Bond waited for the next signal he thought that a heart switch looked obvious, and his finger hovered over the deuce. Meanwhile, back on the submarine, Zia had other ideas, and told him to choose the ♡J. When Stavros covered, Colette won with the ace and returned the ♡4.

Stavros did his best. He advanced the ♣9, and covered with dummy's ten. Bond won and cleared the hearts. In later with the ♣A, he produced the ♡6 for the setting trick.

"Now, Stavros." Saladin was silkily menacing. "You may explain why Zia played the jack of hearts – the only card to defeat you."

Stavros took an anguished breath, and replied in a flat monotone. "The lead of a spade would give me time to establish a club entry to the table. A switch to a low heart would allow me to play the deuce and force out the ace." He took out a handkerchief and mopped his brow feverishly. "Now a heart return from Colette would give me three tricks in that suit, as well as the time to create that club entry. A club return would create one sooner and a spade or a diamond sooner still. Need I go on?"

"Very good, Stavros," said Bond. "But 'sheer genius' would have been shorter."

"W.E.L.L. S.P.O.T.T.E.D." his spectacles told him.

Soon afterwards Colette made an easy heart game to clinch the rubber, and Bond cut Stavros for the next. Saladin opened his account with a finely judged five clubs, and Bond replied with an off-centre four spades. Then Stavros made a hair-raising three no trumps.

"Four successful finesses," Saladin shook his head in mock admiration. "Thank you, Stavros, for providing us with such cliff-hanging excitement. Also for sparing me the indignity of being the victim of a blindingly obvious throw-in." He stood up, leaving lesser mortals to add up the score. "Now let us go into dinner, where you, Stavros, can have second helpings for being so nice to me."

The dining room matched the opulence of the rest of the villa. Cézanne on the walls, Cellini on the table. Served in a restaurant, the dinner would have compelled Michelin to introduce a fourth star. It started with Beluga caviar and then got expensive. They drank the kind of wine the Rothschilds would have kept for themselves. Bond sparkled, Colette glowed, Saladin mellowed. Even Stavros was moved to attempt what for him was probably small talk.

"Your line of play in that five diamonds contract." He wagged his head in sorrowful incredulity. "It was six to four against."

"I believe you, Stavros." Bond sipped his noble claret. "But haven't you heard that life is a pile of six to four against?"

Saladin said, "Stavros bets only on certainties. He has much too much financial expertise to bet on life."

"Or horse sense," Bond said.

Colette, the perfect hostess, was on hand with the perfect feed line. "Why horse sense, Zia?"

"Because horses are far too clever to bet on what people will do."

Saladin seemed amused. The smug bastard hadn't heard that one before. He may have been the bee's knees on Marcel Proust, but he was a washout on Damon Runyon. One up to 007.

"I hope the food is to your liking, Zia," Saladin said.

"Superb," Bond mumbled through a mouth full of truffles. "French is the only truly civilised cuisine."

"Although Chinese has its moments," Colette offered.

"Perhaps," said Saladin. "But I can not take seriously a meal cooked by people who eat with knitting needles."

Once again Colette was right on the ball. "Italian can be marvellous."

"True," agreed Saladin. "But one feels hungry again a week later."

Bond smiled dutifully, but said nothing. He had just realised his exaggerated praise of French food was right out of character, but at least the conversation hadn't turned to curry.

The banquet climaxed with a triumphant cognac. Bond sensed that the blood content in his alcohol was unacceptably high, so he had three. He didn't have to be a model of sobriety, as long as Zia was.

Eventually Saladin rose and said, "I always take a short walk after dining. Perhaps you would like to join me, Zia?"

Bond accepted – it was just what he wanted. "Actually, I would like to see some more of this wonderful house."

"By all means," said Saladin, and the conducted tour began.

As they trod Persian carpets of untold antiquity, Bond was only half aware of Saladin's eloquent discourse. He was concentrating on what he was not being shown. They were about to pass a door which, architecturally speaking, shouldn't have been there. With gauche innocence, he asked, "What's in there?"

"Nothing very interesting, Zia?" Saladin's shrewd dark eyes seemed to bore into Bond's soul. "Why?"

Bond summoned a desperate effort at nonchalance. "Only that it appears to lead into the side of the hill."

"It does. How observant of you." He regarded Bond with a new curiosity. "It is an entrance to our waste disposal plant. Urban dwellers like you are apt to take their civic services for granted. On Saladinos, we need to be self-sufficient."

"Fascinating." Bond nodded respectfully. "Earlier we were discussing power. Does yours derive from self-sufficiency?"

"Hardly, my friend. Self-sufficiency is one of the products. Money is the source."

Bond couldn't resist the urge to stir things up a little. He said, "Yet I've heard that the ability to do without riches is power."

Saladin's lips curled contemptuously. He said, "So have I, often. And invariably from poor people."

Bond managed to resist the urge to strangle him, but it was a close run thing.

They had reached the bridge room, where the other two players were already seated at the table. Bond partnered Saladin for the first rubber.

Love All. Dealer South.

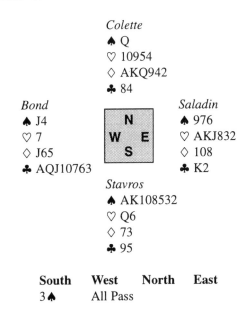

Colette
♠ Q
♡ 10954
◇ AKQ942
♣ 84

Bond
♠ J4
♡ 7
◇ J65
♣ AQJ10763

Saladin
♠ 976
♡ AKJ832
◇ 108
♣ K2

Stavros
♠ AK108532
♡ Q6
◇ 73
♣ 95

South	West	North	East
3♠	All Pass		

Bond began with his singleton heart. After winning with the king, Saladin sat motionless for half a minute before switching to the ♣2. Bond manfully concealed his irritation that hearts were not continued and got ready to win with his ♣10. When he received instructions to play the *ace* and continue with the queen, he was beyond surprise. Saladin perforce overtook with the ♣K, cashed the ♡K for the defence's fourth trick, and fired a deadly low heart.

It wasn't Stavros' day. His face looked as if it had just sucked a lemon as he ruffed high and crossed to dummy's ♠Q. But as Bond had discarded two diamonds on his partner's hearts, the bald man could not return to hand to draw the last trump. He stared accusingly at his tormentor.

He said, "Your play of the ace of clubs was spectacular, but not efficient."

"M.O.R.O.N." observed Bond's spectacles. He hoped Zia was referring to Stavros.

Saladin gave Stavros a condescending smile, and said. "I agree that my partner could have won with a lower card. But in case my club deuce had been a singleton, he wanted to be sure I ruffed the second round."

One page behind, as usual, Bond was just beginning to appreciate the brilliance of his partner's play. "Thank you, Saladin," he smiled, "but you aren't doing justice to your own defence."

"It was nothing." The tall man shrugged. "It was necessary to cash two rounds of clubs before playing hearts, or Stavros would have been able to discard a club." He was didactic, arrogant, infuriating. "I would have attempted to recover by cashing the king of clubs, but too late. He would simply ruff the next heart high. Then he could cross to dummy's queen of trumps and return to hand by ruffing a club."

Bond nodded, like a man who'd been one page ahead from the outset. "I know, partner," he grinned. "I've got the T-shirt."

Colette's spontaneous laugh was cut short by a look of pure malevolence from Saladin. She lowered her eyes in contrition, but Bond was sure he could detect a different emotion.

It was fear.

The tension heightened. After some fiercely competitive auctions, both sides had scored heavily above the line when a part-score deal showed Saladin at his lovable best.

Love All. Dealer South.

Bond
♠ K7
♡ K1093
◇ 1032
♣ J964

Stavros
♠ Q962
♡ 76
◇ A854
♣ Q85

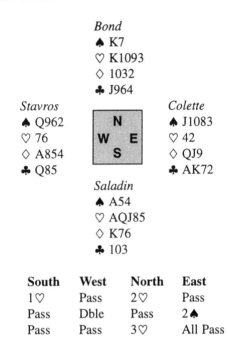

Colette
♠ J1083
♡ 42
◇ QJ9
♣ AK72

Saladin
♠ A54
♡ AQJ85
◇ K76
♣ 103

South	West	North	East
1♡	Pass	2♡	Pass
Pass	Dble	Pass	2♠
Pass	Pass	3♡	All Pass

A spade was led against the three heart contract. It wasn't the best dummy Bond could have put down, but Saladin thanked him politely. He briskly eliminated spades and drew trumps. Now his only concern was to make nine tricks even if the diamond ace was offside. He led ♣3 towards the table. Stavros stolidly followed low and the nine was headed by Colette's king. After a little thought, she correctly returned a low club.

Forced to win with the ♣Q, Stavros could see that a spade would present declarer with a ruff and discard, so he led the eight of clubs. Sneering arrogantly, Saladin played low from dummy. Colette could now calculate that if her partner was left on play he would be forced to open up the diamonds, so she coolly overtook with the ♣A and advanced a deceptive ◇J. Saladin gave her a sardonic nod of approval before playing low, but now, however she continued, the contract was secure.

"Nothing we could do partner," Stavros remarked gracelessly.

"Except insert your ♣8 on the first round," Saladin suggested helpfully.

"Not easy to see," Stavros complained.

"Evidently not." Saladin's smile was pure condescension.

Bond said nothing, but he could see that the ♣8 was the correct play. He and his magic spectacles would have found it! Then, as if in agreement, an unsolicited signal tickled his left ear – T.C. The ten of clubs? But why? Saladin had held that card. Bond pushed his brain into top gear, ignored the rusty rattle of protest, and came up with the answer - Saladin should have led it, instead of the careless club three. He'd got the bastard by the short and curlies! Well spotted, Zia!

He said, "That would certainly have enabled Stavros to escape the end play." Then he moved in for the kill. "Perhaps, for that reason, Saladin, you might have led the club ten."

Suddenly the atmosphere was electric, as Saladin evaluated this treasonable suggestion. By god he was evil! Then he turned slowly towards Bond, smiling only with his mouth.

"How right you are, partner," he said. "Then there would have been no escape."

"It wasn't easy to see though," said Bond ironically, mimicking Stavros.

"You are very kind, Zia, but quite unnecessarily so. Had you been in Stavros' seat, I hope I should have found the club ten. *You* are an opponent worthy of my steel."

Thanks for nothing, Bond thought, but he managed a gracious nod, and the tension eased. Two utterly ruthless men had taken each other's measure and tacitly agreed to postpone their duel.

For a while at least.

Bond knew that criticising Saladin had been the act of an idiot. No, Zia had suggested it by signalling T.C. That made it two idiots. Would the next deal give them a chance to get back into the ego-maniac's good books?

Love All. Dealer North.

Stavros
♠ –
♡ AK654
◇ A65
♣ AQJ103

Saladin
♠ 872
♡ J73
◇ J103
♣ K652

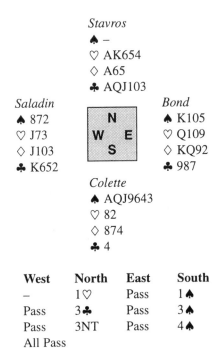

Bond
♠ K105
♡ Q109
◇ KQ92
♣ 987

Colette
♠ AQJ9643
♡ 82
◇ 874
♣ 4

West	North	East	South
–	1♡	Pass	1♠
Pass	3♣	Pass	3♠
Pass	3NT	Pass	4♠
All Pass			

Saladin led the ◇J. Colette viewed dummy's spade void without enthusiasm. She took on the table and continued with ♣A and ♣Q, discarding a diamond. When the defence played two more rounds of diamonds, she ruffed low, and cashed the ♠A, intending, if nothing happened, to continue with the spade queen. At this point, Bond was lazily fingering the ♠5 when he received a contrary instruction from Zia. "T.S!" His was not to reason why, he mused, and just managed to drop the ten in tempo. Now the maniac on the submarine really had gone too far!

Colette paused to sip champagne and take stock. It occurred to her that if she continued with ♠Q and East held the king, a diamond continuation would lead to a fatal trump promotion if Saladin had started with ♠8752. So, not unreasonably, she chose a small spade. Disaster!

"A most ingenious deception, Zia." Saladin was elated. "And there was little danger of its backfiring. Even if Colette had held eight spades to the ace-queen-nine, your play of the ten would have induced her to play a small spade to my now bare jack. I congratulate you."

"Yes," agreed Colette. "It was extremely clever."

"T.O.L.D. Y.O.U." the magic glasses buzzed gleefully.

The rest of the bridge was as exciting as brown Windsor soup. Bond and Zia had agreed a signal to save time in the play. The letter X indicated that the deal was routine, and Bond could play what he liked.

That night saw a plague of X's. Eventually even Saladin had had enough. "One more rubber like that will drive us all into the arms of Morpheus," he announced. He rose pompously. Bond shuddered. He could tell there was another epigram coming, but there was nowhere to hide.

"We were spoiled by the excitement of the earlier hands," Saladin said. "Let us console ourselves with the knowledge that on occasion boredom is a sign of intelligence. Thoreau."

"****! Harold Robbins," muttered Bond, but very much under his breath.

5
Colette

Alone in his room, Bond changed rapidly into fighting kit, and viewed himself in the triple mirrors by his bed. On a childish impulse, he arranged them to create an endless row of Zia-type Bonds.

The result was awesome. A lean body, miraculously restored to the vigour of middle-age, and every inch of it lethal. Rubber-soled shoes with bone-crushing toe caps. Dark Jaeger slacks with belt by Armani and hidden extras by Q. Black leather jacket concealing his powerful arsenal.

Reluctantly, he walked away from the mirrors. The Bond army vanished into the infinite, while its sole survivor edged into the corridor, down the marble staircase and towards the door that led into the forbidden hillside.

As far as he could tell, he wasn't observed. Why should he be? Saladin's security was designed to keep people off the island, not to monitor the people on it. Especially when the only guest was so utterly above suspicion.

He reached his destination and found that the door was still there. He'd half expected that the devil had had it bricked up. There were two yale locks, but Q's gadgets made short work of them. The door opened on to a narrow staircase leading down into the hill-face. He took a deep breath to steady his nerves, and began his reluctant descent, one cautious step at a time. The locks on the door at the bottom were child's play. As it opened, he saw that his search was ended. This was the nerve centre of Saladinos; a room no more than ten feet square, but with more control panels than the Starship Enterprise.

Bond was about to step inside when a strange inner voice told him not to. He felt about as secure as a turkey, sitting on a pile of sage and onion stuffing and listening to Chrismas carols. He sped back up the stairs and into the corridor. He quickly closed the door and strolled towards his room, just as a couple of the ubiquitous Greek wrestlers came into view. They were making for the control room.

Whistling nonchalantly, but with heart thumping, he forced himself to nod casually. They responded with equal indifference. So his fear that they were after him was just another example of his occupational paranoia. He recalled another of the service psychologist's theories: that every agent had a limited deposit at an imaginary courage bank. And Bond had an overdraft as big as the national debt.

Then he nearly jumped out of his skin when a voice behind him called, "Zia!" He whirled around, to see Colette, dressed in a flimsy negligee and posing erotically in the doorway of a room he had just passed. He wondered whether to step inside when a strange inner voice told him it was a bloody good idea.

"Perhaps you'd like to join me for a nightcap," she said.

"Perhaps I would."

Colette closed the door behind him, glided towards the Louis Quinze bed, and produced a magnum of champagne from an ice bucket on the bedroom table.

"You said you liked Tattinger."

"Don't tell me you were expecting me."

"No, Zia, but I'd never tasted Tattinger. I hoped to find we had something in common besides bridge."

"And have we?"

"Let's see." She poured two glasses. They performed the absurd rituals of expert tasting. She said, "I would describe this as a wine Saladin's merely aspires to be."

Bond's eyes widened theatrically. "Do I detect the seeds of treason?"

"I occasionally feel an irrestible urge to mutiny." She sat on the bed, looking anything but mutinous. "I confess I sometimes find Saladin a bit much."

"That's a third item we have in common." Bond sat gingerly beside her. You had to sit gingerly when your jacket and pants contained enough explosives to destroy Liechtenstein. He said, "I wonder what the fourth will be?"

"I'm sure we'll soon find out." She crossed her legs seductively. "But first you must tell me one of your secrets."

"Anything," he lied.

"In that last rubber, why did you take that unbelievably risky diamond finesse?"

"Instinct."

"No, you thought for some time. It was calculated."

He remembered another snippet from his basic training manual. When you're being interrogated, always tell as much of the truth as possible. He said, "A little voice in my ear told me you had it."

"Be serious, Zia."

Sister, if you only knew, he thought. He recalled the deal, but Zia's reasoning was a mystery to him. What now? He was wearing his radio transmitter, so whoever was listening in the submarine would already have called Zia. But to receive Zia's explanation he needed his glasses, and what red-blooded man would put glasses on to seduce a beautiful woman? To hell with it, he thought, and took them from his inside pocket.

"Zia, surely you don't need those to remember a bridge deal."

"You know what they say. Ladies make passes at men who wear glasses."

"You've got it wrong." She laughed musically. "Ladies make passes, but after two glasses. So pour me another one please."

Bond did the honours, while he concentrated on the dots and dashes which were coming through at a rate of knots. Zia, at last, was on the job.

Game All. Dealer South.

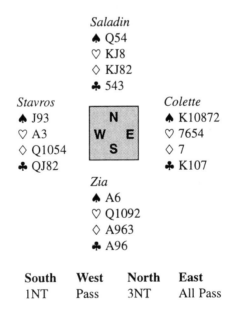

Saladin
♠ Q54
♡ KJ8
◇ KJ82
♣ 543

Stavros
♠ J93
♡ A3
◇ Q1054
♣ QJ82

Colette
♠ K10872
♡ 7654
◇ 7
♣ K107

Zia
♠ A6
♡ Q1092
◇ A963
♣ A96

South	West	North	East
1NT	Pass	3NT	All Pass

Bond recalled that Zia had told him to open a strong no trump, probably because he had three of his beloved nines.

"W.C.L.E.D," the glasses reminded him cryptically.

"Stavros led the two of clubs," Bond reminded Colette.

""I know," she reminded him, a little petulantly. "I was there."

"I held off for two rounds," he stalled, and expertly kissed the nape of her exquisite neck.

"Then you led a heart towards dummy," said Colette, her breath quickening. "Stavros went in with the ace."

"He cashed the fourth club," Bond whispered, nibbling her ear while he deciphered the signals buzzing furiously in his own. "He exited with ... a heart ... and I cashed ... my heart winners."

"Now you played your ace of diamonds – oh, this is so sexy," she breathed, "and a low diamond ... towards the table."

"Yes," he nibbled. "All strictly routine."

"Until you won the trick with your *eight*."

"Elementary, my dear ... Colette." He transferred his attack to her other ear. "I took the deep diamond finesse for two reasons. Which ... would you ... like first?"

"The second one," she gasped.

"A wise choice. Stavros was almost as likely to hold queen-ten to four as queen to three .... There are three ... combinations of each."

"I believe you, darling. So let's skip the other reason."

Bond was dying to skip it, but he'd spent three mind-bending minutes decoding Zia's rationale, and wasn't going to waste them.

He said, "Stavros was more likely to lead from a four card major than a four card minor."

"Damn Stavros!" she giggled.

"He had shown up with a doubleton heart," he persisted cruelly. "So his likely shape was ... three ... two ... four ... four."

"Oh, Zia," she said wistfully. "I wonder if I'll ever be able to play like you."

"You will in time." He returned, impartially, to the original ear. "All you need is twenty years of alcohol, late nights and sex."

"It sounds delicious. When do you think I should start?"

"Well, it's gone two o'clock. We've had a lot of champagne." He placed the glasses on the bedside table. Then, as an afterthought, he made sure they were pointing away from the bed. "The third ingredient is seriously overdue."

At last Bond was on the job ....

Some time later, as they lay on the bed, Colette lit a cigarette, while Bond moved closer in a covert attempt to indulge in some secondary smoking.

"I didn't know you smoked," he said, between surreptitious inhalations.

"Not in front of Saladin." She turned towards him and exhaled luxuriantly. "And I didn't know you did."

"I don't."

"Yes, you do. Every time I blow in your direction, you gulp air like a drowning man third time up."

"OK, officer. It's a fair cop. I'm a closet smoker."

"And another thing, darling. You don't need glasses, do you?"

He held his breath. This was getting dangerous. "What makes you think that?"

"I tried them on when you dozed off just now. Zero magnification."

"I confess. They are purely for vanity, to make me look more intelligent."

"And they do, darling." She traced her finger along a faint scar on his right forearm. "But the effect is spoiled by the battle scars. No wonder you refused to undress. Even so, I could tell you've been in the wars. I'd no idea playing bridge was so dangerous."

"It isn't." Bond made a valiant attempt to sound natural. "Outraged husbands and jealous women are dangerous."

"You needn't bother to keep up the pretence. And you needn't worry about Saladin finding out. I'm not going to tell him."

"Tell him what, Colette?"

"That you're not Zia." She lit another cigarette and put it between his lips. He hungrily devoured the soothing smoke, as his brain raced to cope with this new factor.

He said, "Alright, Colette. Tell me what else you've deduced."

Colette said, "For some months, I've suspected that Saladin has been planning something very big, and very illegal. I must admit I've been scared."

"Why haven't you left him?"

"He doesn't like people leaving him." She gave a little shiver. "He says it's bad for their health."

"Go on." He was too busy smoking to make any comment.

"I believe you're some sort of agent, sent to stop him. But your act is terribly good. Are you from *Mission Impossible*?"

He studied her for a few moments, and made his decision. He said, "Colette, the story I'm going to tell you is so incredible that ...."

"Is it a long one?"

"Well, fairly."

"Then let's make love while you tell it."

6
Exposure

Next morning, James Bond woke at the crack of noon. He picked up his bedside telephone and brazenly ordered breakfast. After a pint of freshly-squeezed orange juice and a quart of black coffee you could stand a spoon in, he felt almost human. In fact, for a man recovering from enough champagne to launch a small fleet, and enough sex to satisfy half its crew, he was a walking miracle.

He took stock. He had passed himself off as Zia without a hitch. Oh yes, there was Colette, but even when he was working under the awesome handicap of a false identity, his legendary sex-appeal had scored again – she had become an ally. The position of Saladin's control room had been transmitted to M. A commando force would invade the island at midnight, but purely as a diversion. As usual, the real work would be down to 007. In the meantime all he had to do, in the words of Noel Coward, was remember his lines and not fall over the furniture.

At two o'clock, looking and feeling immaculate, Bond strolled into the cardroom, where Colette and Stavros were waiting. At one minute past, Saladin entered with supreme confidence, a white vision of splendour. He smiled at Bond like an emperor greeting his favourite gladiator. We who are about to die salute you, Bond thought wryly, while vowing that if anyone was going to die it was Saladin.

They cut for partners. Bond drew Colette. The bridge was undistinguished. He went down in an over-ambitious three no trumps. Stavros suffered a tongue-lashing from his partner for a phantom sacrifice. Then Saladin failed in an easy six spades, yet managed to give the impression he had played like a master.

Then the Morse signals stopped!

It happened on Bond's deal, while he was wondering whether to open two no trumps. A minute passed. He muttered the code word which would tell Zia that transmission had ceased, but when nothing happened, he realised he was on his own. They're all out to get me, he fumed, even Q. But so what? He had twenty points and a good five card suit. To hell with the doubleton club – he'd show them all.

"One heart," he said timidly.

Love All. Dealer South.

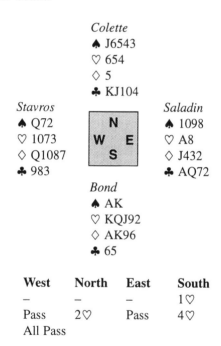

Colette
♠ J6543
♡ 654
◇ 5
♣ KJ104

Stavros
♠ Q72
♡ 1073
◇ Q1087
♣ 983

Saladin
♠ 1098
♡ A8
◇ J432
♣ AQ72

Bond
♠ AK
♡ KQJ92
◇ AK96
♣ 65

West	North	East	South
–	–	–	1♡
Pass	2♡	Pass	4♡
All Pass			

Stavros led the ♣8 to the jack and queen. Saladin continued with the ♣A and was disappointed at the appearance of his partner's nine. Seeing no attractive alternative, he played a third round of clubs. This is like shelling peas, thought Bond, as he discarded a diamond and promptly continued with the ◇A and a diamond ruff.

He now played a trump to the king. When this held it suddenly dawned on him that there was a risk of running into a trump promotion. The longer he thought about it the greater the danger seemed. He prayed for the Morse signals to return. Nothing! Finally he tried a *low* trump and was rewarded when Saladin sourly produced the ace. Bond felt ten feet tall! Now he could afford to ruff the fourth round of clubs high. Zia, eat your heart out, he thought triumphantly.

As he proudly recorded the score, the signals, now that he no longer needed them, began again. "L.U.C.K.Y. B.A.S.T.A.R.D." Lucky? He seethed. Luck had nothing to do with it. The going had got tough and the tough had got going. And that was one in the eye for M, for daring to suggest that Bond was over the hill.

Anyway, Saladin seemed to approve. He gazed searchingly at Bond and said, "What an extraordinary line."

Bond swiftly changed his facial expression from smug to modest. "Oh, I don't know," he shrugged. "It was nothing really."

"It certainly was nothing." Saladin shook his head in disbelief. "You were forced to play against the odds to foil a trump promotion. Had you played a trump from the table before tackling diamonds, the anti-percentage play would not have become necessary."

Bond was up the unmentionable creek without a paddle, and he knew it. He hadn't drawn trumps soon enough, and now he was stuck on the bloody embankment, knee-deep in mixed metaphors. Typically, he fought back with true British grit.

"Forgive my memory, Saladin." He smothered an imaginary yawn. "But didn't I make the contract?"

"Indeed you did." Saladin responded with an ironic bow. "In a manner worthy of the Rueful Rabbit. That in itself is unremarkable. Some of the world's finest players have made worse errors at this very table. But the classic definition of an expert is one who can identify the right line immediately after chosing the wrong one. It was your failure to do that which finally convinced me that you are not Zia Mahmood."

At that moment, two wrestlers entered. Saladin must have signalled. Probably a McKenney, Bond thought hysterically.

"The hand illustrates a fairly common theme," Saladin said. "It effectively distinguishes the average player from the expert."

Bond struggled to keep a snarl off his face. That was the same rotten thing M had said. It wasn't fair. Wherever he went there was always a bloody authority figure who made him feel like a naughty little boy. He sat and sulked while the Greek tag team searched him, and glanced at the other players. Stavros was goggling at him like a startled halibut. Colette looked as if her eyes were trying to tell him something. But what? There was no time to find out – Saladin was in full flow.

"I was intrigued when you showed an inexplicable curiosity about an innocent-looking door."

Saladin looked, without curiosity, at the pile of innocent-looking objects his wrestlers had taken from Bond's pockets. Bond noted that they had overlooked his display handkerchief with the miniature transmitter.

"When I heard that you were seen in that vicinity at two o'clock this morning, Saladin added drily, I really began to wonder."

Bond let that one sail over the baseline. He had a hunch a cannon ball was on its way. It was.

"I must admit that until ten minutes ago you played like the real Zia. Except for your tempo. Those minute hesitations, accompanied by the brief, but visible mental exertions, were sadly out of character."

"It's results that count," Bond wriggled. "You can put the pauses down to too much champagne.

"Really?" said Saladin. "And the last deal?"

"Surely everyone's entitled to one mistake."

"But you made two, my friend."

Bond decided to say nothing. He knew enough to quit when he was behind.

Saladin noted his blank expression and said. "Do you recall my unsuccessful spade slam?"

"Yes," said Bond. "My defence was routine, but adequate."

"But your performance in the post mortem was bovine."

"T.I.C.K." the spectacles agreed annoyingly.

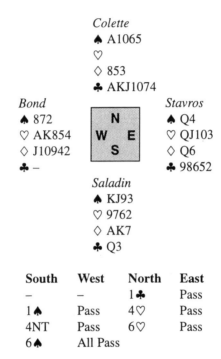

Colette
- ♠ A1065
- ♡
- ◊ 853
- ♣ AKJ1074

Bond
- ♠ 872
- ♡ AK854
- ◊ J10942
- ♣ –

Stavros
- ♠ Q4
- ♡ QJ103
- ◊ Q6
- ♣ 98652

Saladin
- ♠ KJ93
- ♡ 9762
- ◊ AK7
- ♣ Q3

South	West	North	East
–	–	1♣	Pass
1♠	Pass	4♡	Pass
4NT	Pass	6♡	Pass
6♠	All Pass		

"You led the ace of hearts. I ruffed on the table and played a trump to the nine, which held. Then I made the master play of a second trump to the ten. Stavros won with the queen and gave you a club ruff to defeat the cast-iron contract."

"Never mind, Saladin." Bond was the picture of sympathy. "I'm told that some of the world's finest players have made worse errors at this very table."

Saladin gave him a pitying look. "You still don't see it, do you? Let me remind you of what I said, that I would have made the contract if you and Stavros had changed seats."

Bond remembered the comment. It meant as little to him now as it did at the time. Saladin had cocked up the hand. Why wouldn't he admit it?

But the man was still droning on. "The real Zia, in the West seat, would have been expert enough, holding queen to four, to duck the first round of trumps. In that case, continuing with the spade ace would have been fatal."

Now Bond could see it! The finesse of the ten was a safety play, which had failed only because of the five-nil club split. But it was too late to say so – Zia would have spotted it at the time.

Saladin was enjoying his distress. "We will now play a game of question and answer," he said. "You will provide the answers."

Bond judged that a spot of grade A defiance was called for. "Don't bet your life on it, Saladin."

"But it is your life which is in the balance." Saladin signalled to one of the wrestlers, who produced a Walther automatic. "You will reply truthfully to each question within three seconds. If you do not, we will shoot off your right ear-lobe, and ask again. Each attempt to procrastinate or prevaricate …" He paused to admire his alliteration. "… will result in the loss of another of your extremities, of which, assuming you are normal, there are twenty-six."

Bond swallowed. It sounded too many, but he didn't feel like counting.

"Question one," announce Saladin. "You are obviously a secret agent. Of which country?"

"I'm British," Bond snapped, with no more than two point-eight seconds to spare.

"Good." Saladin was satisfied, and Bond was relieved. His right ear-lobe wasn't his favourite extremity, but he was attached to it.

"Now," said Saladin. "We can omit the question why you are on Saladinos, since the answer is obvious. I am far more intrigued to find out how you managed, even sporadically, to play bridge like Zia."

Strictly speaking, this wasn't a question, but Bond was taking no chances. "My glasses," he said.

"What about them?"

"For one thing, when I wear them I can see through the backs of the cards." Bond had just had a crazy idea. So crazy it might even succeed.

"I don't believe you," said Saladin. But there was a note of doubt in his voice.

"Do you think I want to lose half an ear? See for yourself." Bond tossed off his glasses and placed them in front of Saladin.

"Very well," Saladin put them on and peered at the backs of several cards. He opened his mouth to speak but was silenced by a command from Bond.

"Don't move, Saladin, or I'll blow your head off."

The tall man showed no emotion, but he was taking no chances. "May I ask how? I can perceive no obvious instrument of destruction."

"You're wearing it." Bond's voice and expression were laden with self-assurance. "Just as I planned you would. Those glasses only contain enough explosive to destroy one extremity. But in your case the extremity concerned is your head."

Suddenly, everyone in the room was perfectly still. Then, the tableau was shattered by Stavros, cravenly edging his chair as far from his employer as possible. Bond didn't fancy his chances at the next salary review.

"Don't worry, Stavros," he said soothingly, you're well out of range."

"You're bluffing." Saladin was still fearless, but cautious. "Where precisely is your detonator?"

Bond carefully raised his right hand to reveal a thumb pushed against the base of his middle finger. "It's my signet ring," he said. "I've already pressed it for the necessary four seconds." He recalled another gem from his basic training – make sure your lies are all big ones, and make them technical. "The explosion will take place the moment I remove my thumb. In the meantime your life, Saladin, depends on the Heisenberg delay mechanism poised delicately on the bridge of your nose."

Sweat glistened on Saladin's forehead, but his voice was commendably steady. "I trust it isn't based on Heisenberg's theory of uncertainty?"

Blast! Bond was shaken, but stirred into a lightning recovery. "Of course," he grinned. "Sometimes it doesn't work."

"How do I know you are not bluffing?"

Good, thought Bond. The cliche proved he'd got the swine rattled. "Why not tell Diogenes here to shoot me?" He looked Saladin coldly in the eye. "Our deaths will be practically simultaneous."

"Not an appetising prospect," Saladin sneered.

"No," Bond agreed. "I too would have chosen different company. So you'd better do exactly as I tell you."

The cruel lips curled. "Do you expect me to obey you?"

Shades of Goldfinger, what an opening! "No, Saladin, I expect you to die."

Saladin gave a thin smile of resignation. "Then I must try my best to disappoint you."

Bond felt so good he wanted to chew the scenery. He'd won hands down! "Tell your people to put their guns on the table," he commanded. "And advise them not to shoot me. If they do, I can't promise to keep my thumb in place."

Saladin spoke rapidly in Greek, and within seconds Bond was admiring an impressive collection of weapons, putting his own back into his pockets and cursing the fact that to maintain the fiction of the exploding spectacles he had to work left-handed. Saladin watched him carefully and said, "My friend, since I can no longer address you as Zia, may I ask your name?"

"Bond."

"Not the famous James Bond? Surely he was put out to grass years ago?"

A sudden wave of anger poured through Bond. He was about to remove his thumb sadistically from the detonator, when he remembered it was all a preposterous hoax. "Reports of my death were somewhat exaggerated," he muttered lamely.

From then on, everything was almost too easy. Some instinct warned him not to reveal that Colette was now on the side of the angels, but he 'recruited' her to help him lock Stavros and the Greeks in the wine cellar. An acquiescent Saladin was shepherded down the staircase and into the control room, where he stoically watched his captor set explosive devices to all the instruments. He meekly revealed the whereabouts of the nuclear bombs and listened while the information was released to the submarine.

Bond felt as if he had just seen the defence present him with an impossible contract. But he had a nagging doubt that it would turn out to be a gigantic hornswoggle.

7
Hornswoggled

James Bond cursed his aching thumb. He decided that applying pressure to a non-existent detonator should be crossed off the list of his top ten leisure activities. He considered dropping the pretence and covering his hostage with a gun. But this hostage was a supreme ego-maniac, who would see a gun as an irresistible challenge. Bond would have to kill him, and, attractive as the idea was, it would destroy the one lever that was keeping Saladin's hit-men at bay. Besides, the situation appealed to his vanity. He was like Zia with his weird discards – even his singletons were deceptive.

They were back in the card room. Colette was calmly playing patience. Saladin was enjoying some of his own-brand champagne while he sat on a sofa and wrote down a bridge deal. Bond was at the window, keeping an eye on his prisoner and the other on a spot in the ocean where he hoped the submarine would surface. This would mean that the nuclear devices had been located and neutralised, and that all good Europeans could sleep tight in their federal beds again. Soon afterwards, a naval helicopter would arrive, to take the three of them off the island.

Of course this all depended on Bond's message having reached the sub. The only way he could receive an acknowledgement was via his glasses. And Saladin was wearing them. So the fate of Western civilisation depended on the reliability of Q's transmitter. Welcome back the Dark Ages, Bond thought sourly.

"Mr Bond," said Saladin, with silky deference, "while we are waiting for the arrival of your transport, you might care to amuse yourself with this hand."

Bond moved towards his captive, stopping two metres away. "I might," he said. "Place it two feet to your right."

Saladin complied. Watching him warily, Bond picked up the piece of paper, and wondered why he was bothering. Perhaps he wanted the chance to show the supercilious snob that he wasn't the palooka he was supposed to be.

Game All. Dealer South.

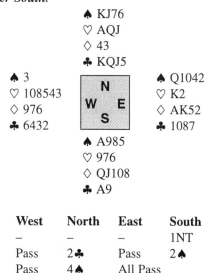

♠ KJ76
♥ AQJ
♦ 43
♣ KQJ5

♠ 3
♥ 108543
♦ 976
♣ 6432

♠ Q1042
♥ K2
♦ AK52
♣ 1087

♠ A985
♥ 976
♦ QJ108
♣ A9

West	North	East	South
–	–	–	1NT
Pass	2♣	Pass	2♠
Pass	4♠	All Pass	

"South opened a somewhat shaded weak no trump." Saladin explained. "His partner decided to settle for game. You, my friend, are East. How would you defend on the lead of the seven of diamonds?"

"Doggedly," Bond replied. He hardly needed to look at all four hands – the deal was double dummy. "After winning the first trick with the king I exit gracefully, and hope declarer gets the trumps wrong."

"Very good, Mr Bond." Saladin's condescension was masterly. "But what if declarer happens to be a bridge player? He will simply play to the spade king, and small towards hand. When a low card appears from East, he will insert the nine. This ensures three tricks against any four-one distribution."

"I realise that." Bond shrugged. Saladin was up to something, but what? "So what exactly is your point?"

"Suppose you took the first trick with the ace, to create the impression that your partner had led from three to the king. Then you make the master play of advancing the heart deuce."

Bond considered this. It was stupid enough to remind him of Zia's signals from the submarine. "Go on," he said.

"Now declarer will read you for a singleton heart. He may eschew the trump safety play and go one down."

Bond nodded. "Very clever," he said.

"Thank you," said Saladin, "I wonder if you can see the connection between that deal and our present situation?"

"Off the top of my head, no."

"It prompted me to give more thought to the contrast between the brilliance of your card play and the feebleness of your analysis."

"Don't tax your brain, Saladin. Life's too short."

"These glasses do not magnify. Nor do they penetrate the backs of the cards." His dark eyes appraised Bond shrewdly. "It follows that they must have other purposes."

"Of course." Bond felt his skin tighten at the groin. "They're explosive."

"So you said. But remember I have since witnessed your broadcast to your confederates. It was strictly one-way. Ergo, you still have your transmitter, but have been recently deprived of your receiver. And the only thing you have relinquished and not recovered is this pair of glasses."

"Excellent, Saladin." Bond had to admire the man. "But how does that change your position.?"

"If my theory is correct, they have to be capable of transmitting visual images, and also receiving verbal responses."

"So?"

"To perform both functions alone they would be a miracle of micro-technology. That they also contain a sophisticated explosive device is a little hard to believe. I suspect that, *like the defender in that problem*, you have projected a danger which doesn't exist."

"O.K, Saladin." Bond prayed that his insolent drawl would conceal his feeling of blind panic. "Try to take them off and watch me release my thumb," he said. "My only regret will be that you'll never hear me say I told you so."

"My dear Mr Bond." Saladin sat back lazily. "I shouldn't dream of risking my life on a theory, even if it were underwritten by Einstein. My curiosity is purely academic."

Bond relaxed. He reinforced the illusion of confidence by holding out the bridge deal. Saladin stretched out a languid hand to accept it. Then, with blinding speed, those long strong fingers were clamped around Bond's left wrist, and their bodies were locked in a life-and-death struggle. Saladin's strategy was brilliant! Their heads were so close that if the glasses had been explosive, Bond wouldn't have dared to detonate them. He would have been fighting one-handed.

But they weren't, and he wasn't. He began to pound Saladin's ribs with his right fist. The tall man laughed triumphantly. He hurled away the harmless spectacles and began to fight like a tiger. Within seconds, Bond was flat on his back and fingers of steel were throttling his life away. He was dimly aware of Colette pointing a gun towards him. It went off. He moaned piteously.

His last conscious thought was that his life had ended with a bang and a whimper.

When Bond woke, he was lying on a couch in the white, antiseptic sick room of a naval submarine. His neck felt as if it had been through a mangle, but he guessed he'd live.

"Ah, 007, you're awake." M was sitting by his side, cheerfully filling his pipe.

"I believe it's no smoking, Sir." Chances to rebuke his chief were rare, and Bond didn't like missing one.

"It is for you, Commander." M started to fill the room with lethal clouds.

"But I'm an admiral."

"Quite, Sir." Bond glanced at his watch. It was only six in the evening.

"You had us worried for a while, James." M's battle-hardened face showed the strain he had been under. "When Saladin hurled those priceless spectacles away we thought they'd been smashed to bits. But they were completely undamaged."

"Q will be pleased, Sir."

"Yes, sorry about the glitch, by the way."

"I understand, Sir. Typical British workmanship."

"It wasn't that, 007. Zia thought the hand was so easy he went out for a natural break. Forgot about the X signal. The girl saved you, of course. Shot Saladin dead just as you passed out. By that time the 'copter had arrived, so we got you both aboard the sub in no time."

"I see, Sir. And Western civilisation?"

"We think it would be a good idea."

"Very witty, Sir." Bond tried not to smile, and succeeded without difficulty. "I meant the nuclear warheads."

"All neutralised. Saladin's control room blew up on schedule. The real Mona Lisa's on her way back to the Louvre. The French have started buying British beef again. All in all, a pretty good show."

Was this a veiled compliment? Bond decided to test the water. "Thanks to Colette and Zia," he fished shamelessly.

"Absolutely," said M. Was there a twinkle in the cold blue eyes? No, Bond decided. The old curmudgeon was as ungrateful as ever.

Bond said, "I'd like to see Colette. To say thanks and all that."

"Hm." M puffed reflectively. "You'll have the opportunity at dinner tonight. Eight o'clock in the ward room. Bit of a celebration."

"And Zia, Sir. I'd like to thank him. There were one or two hands I could never have managed without him."

"Not now, 007. If I were you I'd leave that till dinner as well."

"Why not now, Sir?" Bond sat up experimentally. His head stayed on, and every muscle was in prime second-class condition. "I'm as fit as a flea, Sir."

"Very well, 007." M let out a sigh of resignation. "Turn left out of the door. Zia's cabin is the third one along. I'll stay here and finish my pipe."

Bond felt on top of the world as he made his way along the gangway. First he'd see Zia. Then he'd have a stiff drink and a cigarette or three. Then he'd go and find Colette. And by God he deserved her!

He arrived at the third door. He was about to knock when he heard a familiar seductive voice from inside the cabin.

"Oh, Zia," the voice said wistfully. "I wonder if I'll ever be able to play like you."

Appendix 2

The number needed to treat

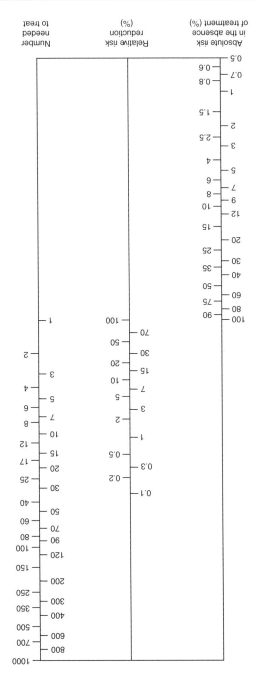

FIGURE Nomogram for calculating the number needed to treat. Published with permission[1]

Clinical Evidence mini CD-ROM

The Clinical Evidence mini CD-ROM allows you to:

- Refer to the full Clinical Evidence content including clinical questions, summary and background information, evidence detail, figures, tables and appendices
- Choose the method of navigation you prefer, through the table of contents, topic sections or the search engine
- Hyperlink references to abstracts where they appear on PubMed and Cochrane (Internet access required)
- Hyperlink to the glossary, figures, tables and references
- Print the full text of any of the 158 topics

To access Clinical Evidence help:

- From within the Clinical Evidence CD-ROM, simply click on the link at the top of the screen or from within Windows, select Programs > Clinical Evidence > Help (if you have already installed Clinical Evidence)
- For technical help, please go to the FAQs at www.clinicalevidence.com
- For damaged CD-ROMs please contact:
  BMJ Publishing Group • Tel: +44(0) 207 383 6270 • subscriptions@bmjgroup.com (UK/ROW)
  For individual subscriptions • Tel: +1 800 373 2897/+1 240 646 7000 • clinevid@pmds.com (USA)
  For individuals receiving Clinical Evidence Concise courtesy of UnitedHealth Foundation:
  ce@unitedhealthfoundation.org

Browsers

Microsoft Internet Explorer 5.5 is the recommended browser, and should be your default browser when installing Clinical Evidence.

This software has been tested with the following browsers:

- Microsoft Internet Explorer 5.0 (English)
- Microsoft Internet Explorer 5.5 (English)
- Microsoft Internet Explorer 6.0 (English)
- Netscape 4.7 (English)
- Netscape 6.0 (English)

Please note

Microsoft Internet Explorer 4 is not a supported browser.

Microsoft Internet Explorer 6 is not compatible with Windows 95.

Internet Explorer 5.5 and 6.0 are available on the installation CD-ROM — see below for details.

To install Microsoft Internet Explorer v5.5

(i) With the Clinical Evidence Installation CD-ROM in the CD-ROM drive, select Run from the Start menu.

(ii) Type d:\other\ie5.5\ie5setup and click OK (where d: is your CD-ROM drive letter).

(iii) Follow the on-screen instructions. The typical installation requires approximately 17 Mbytes of hard disk space.

To install Microsoft Internet Explorer v6.0

(i) With the Clinical Evidence Installation CD-ROM in the CD-ROM drive, select Run from the Start menu.

(ii) Type d:\other\ie6.0\ie6setup and click OK (where d: is your CD-ROM drive letter).

(iii) Follow the on-screen instructions. The typical installation requires approximately 25 Mbytes of hard disk space.

To install Adobe Acrobat Reader v5.0.5

(i) With the Clinical Evidence Installation CD-ROM in the CD-ROM drive, select Run from the Start menu.

(ii) Type d:\Adobe\ar505enu and click OK (where d: is your CD-ROM drive letter).

(iii) Follow the on-screen instructions.

To install Clinical Evidence

(i) Exit from any Windows programs you have running.

(ii) Insert the Clinical Evidence Installation CD-ROM into the CD-ROM drive. The installation starts automatically (if it does not, select Run from the Start menu and enter d:\setup (where d: is your CD-ROM drive letter).

(iii) Follow the on-screen instructions. As part of this process, you can install Adobe Acrobat Reader so you can efficiently print Clinical Evidence topics — this can also be installed later by following the instructions below. An additional 20 Mbytes of hard disk space is required for this.

Minimum system requirements

An IBM compatible PC with at least this specification:

- 60 Mbytes hard disk space
- 90 MHz processor
- 32 MBytes of RAM
- CD-ROM drive
- Modem, if you want to access the Internet for updates, etc.
- SVGA monitor recommended

Operating systems

This software has been tested with the following operating systems:

- Microsoft Windows 95
- Microsoft Windows 98
- Microsoft Windows 2000 Professional
- Microsoft Windows XP Professional
- Microsoft Windows NT SP6
- Microsoft Windows 2000 Server

Please note

Windows XP Home Edition is not a supported operating system. However, please refer to the Windows XP Home section in the Readme file, which is located:

Start > Programs > Clinical Evidence > Readme (if you have already installed Clinical Evidence) or contact technical help.

This CD-ROM has been thoroughly tested for viruses at all stages of production. However, we recommend that you always run a virus checker on any new software before running it. The BMJ Publishing Group cannot accept responsibility for any disruption, damage or loss to your data or computer system that may occur while using this CD-ROM, the programs or data on it.